First, Best

Best

LESSONS IN LEADERSHIP AND LEGACY
FROM TODAY'S CIVIL RIGHTS MOVEMENT

STEVEN L. REED

WITH FAGAN HARRIS

Avery
an imprint of Penguin Random House
New York

AVERY

an imprint of Penguin Random House LLC
penguinrandomhouse.com

Most Avery books are available at special quantity discounts for bulk purchase for sales promotions, premiums, fund-raising, and educational needs. Special books or book excerpts also can be created to fit specific needs. For details, write SpecialMarkets@penguinrandomhouse.com.

Library of Congress Cataloging-in-Publication Data

Names: Reed, Steven L., author. | Harris, Fagan, author.
Title: First, best: lessons in leadership and legacy from today's civil rights movement / Steven Reed with Fagan Harris.
Other titles: Lessons in leadership and legacy from today's civil rights movement
Description: New York: Avery, an imprint of Penguin Random House, [2023]
Identifiers: LCCN 2023005620 (print) | LCCN 2023005621 (ebook) |
ISBN 9780593421758 (hardcover) | ISBN 9780593421765 (epub)
Subjects: LCSH: Reed, Steven L. | Reed, Joe L. | African American mayors—Alabama—Montgomery—Biography. | Mayors—Alabama—Montgomery—Biography. | Civil rights movements—Alabama—Montgomery—History. | African American civil rights workers—Alabama—Montgomery—Biography. | Civil rights workers—Alabama—Montgomery—Biography. | Montgomery (Ala.)—Biography.
Classification: LCC F334.M753 A27 2023 (print) | LCC F334.M753 (ebook) |
DDC 976.1/47092 [B]—dc23/eng/20230419
LC record available at https://lccn.loc.gov/2023005620
LC ebook record available at https://lccn.loc.gov/2023005621

Printed in the United States of America
1st Printing

Book design by Shannon Nicole Plunkett

Some names and identifying characteristics have been changed to protect the privacy of the individuals involved.

To Kyla, Joe Klein, and Karsten:
Thank you for the honor, and experience, of Fatherhood.
May this book serve as a guidepost to you
for many years to come.

Contents

Chapter 1

ORIGINS

I trace my political awakening back to my father's Viking blue 1982 Oldsmobile 98. He proudly called it his "company car," a classic. My dad loved the broad chassis, the long hood, and the way it rode close to the ground. More importantly, he loved how *he* felt when he was in the car: impenetrable. "It rides like a cruise ship," he would remark. To hear my dad tell it, if Shaft had gone into politics, he would have driven an Oldsmobile 98.

My dad, Joe Reed, was fanatical about his Oldsmobile. For starters, he banished my brother and me from sitting in the front passenger seat. It was always the back seat for us. And he insisted on parking it in the garage. When he returned home from work, there was no running to greet him in the driveway. He was insistent: "Unless I am in the car with you, stay out of it."

Understood.

Throughout my childhood, my father wore many hats, professionally, but his North Star was always the same: politicking, persuading, and pushing America to live up to her founding creed that people all are created equal and endowed by their creator with certain inalienable rights, including life, liberty, and the pursuit of happiness.

My father's life work is the project of American democracy. From his own personal life experience and a career dedicated to advancing civil rights, my father understood the vast chasm that exists between what America says she is "on paper," and the lived reality of many of its citizens, especially those of us who are Black.[1] He always understood what many today are only now beginning to realize: American democracy is both fallible and fragile, and without constant vigilance we risk losing it.

My dad's story begins in the Alabama Black Belt.

There, large cotton plantations and sharecroppers kept small tenant farmers, just like my dad's family, barely subsisting. My dad was born in the heart of the Black Belt, in Conecuh County, which is closer in every sense to Biloxi, Mississippi, than to Birmingham, Alabama, if that tells you anything. Even today, it's a little bit like stepping back in time when you drive through that part of the state. Agriculture, and its surrounding culture, still dictate life's terms: people are self-sufficient and mostly keep to themselves. Long dirt roads and vast tracks of fields filled with puffy white cotton mark the landscape.

There's an uneasy sense that one should stick to the roads and places they know. It's not a place to wander.

My dad spent the first eighteen years of his life here, in the Black Belt. His mother's mantra, when my dad was growing up, was "Don't get in any trouble." And she'd follow that piece of advice with a more ominous warning: "If you get in any trouble, *I can't help you*. So don't get in any trouble."

This was the era of Emmett Till. These were the years when a young Black boy could be brutally murdered for being in the wrong place at the wrong time.

My grandmother, my father's mother, was a quiet Christian woman who worked her entire life as a domestic when she wasn't working the family farm. She understood the environment in which they lived and did everything a good mother would do in that situation: she kept her children close and out of harm's way by doling out discipline and a regimen of hard, often backbreaking work on the family farm.

The Black Belt reverberates with that painful history. When you dig into the soil and the people who farm it, you discover what has animated the Black journey across American history.

First, it wasn't too long ago that most Americans depended on agriculture for everything. For generations of Black Americans, farming was all we ever knew since our forced migration to this land centuries ago. As a boy, my dad worked the family farm. Like his parents, and their parents, and *their parents*, my dad toiled under the oppressively hot Alabama sun to till soil darker than the night. They planted cotton and corn, peas and pecans. My dad plowed with mules. He was even a lumberjack one summer.

In the 1940s, life in the Black Belt wasn't too far removed from life in the 1880s. The environment and living conditions reflected that: no running water or indoor plumbing, dirt roads as far as the eye could see, and communities of humble homes held together by clay, rudimentary tools, and hard hands.

Second, and more importantly, Black Alabamians—as was the case for most Black Americans then—lived as second-class citizens in what was a deeply segregated society. Segregation dictated *everything* about our lives: where we could call home, work, or go to school, who we could socialize with, and even who we could *marry.*

Segregation shaped opportunity, too: who had it, who didn't. For Black and white families alike, education was incredibly important. The knowledge economy was emerging, and "head knowledge" was increasingly important if you wanted to escape the farm. And while most white families didn't lack for educational options, most Black families had access to only one school, if they were lucky. Access was an issue, as the one school was usually miles and miles away from most Black families. Later, after the war, Black veterans would drive their newly purchased cars across the South to offer rides to young Black children trying to get to and from school. There were no school buses.

Indeed, if a Black community *wanted* a school, then they had to fund its construction *on their own* and just open it. *Only then* would the public school system send a teacher to run the school and teach classes. Meanwhile, white schools, many of which had been open for decades, saw their construction funded by the state. They received the latest textbooks, enjoyed organized sports, and were guided to the local workforce system.

In high school, my dad learned just how different Black education was from white education. He attended the Conecuh County Training School. The word *training* was used because folks then didn't see Black people as educated; rather, they were simply to be trained to do different things. In education, vocational agriculture was the focus. The state assumed that Black people were good for only menial labor. The laws in place at the time required that Black communities have access only to training manuals—and never books. The prevailing attitude then was that Black people needed to be "trained," just like a horse that needed to be trained to listen.

That system of segregation survived—indeed, *thrived*—on Black political disenfranchisement. To put it in perspective, for the first three decades of my father's life, Black people in the South just didn't vote.

Not that some of us weren't technically *allowed* to. We earned that right after the Civil War, when the "Reconstruction Amendments" of the U.S. Constitution abolished slavery (except for those "duly convicted" of a crime), enshrined due process and equal protection under the law, and established the constitutional right to vote (but for men only; white women would wait another fifty years and Black women would only secure the right a full century later).

But if I've learned anything from my father's story, it's this: history *never* marches in a straight line; it zigs and zags.[2] In the fight for change, our society tends to take a few tentative steps forward before the occasional leap backward. You don't need to look far to confirm that this is indeed the case—in the fifteen years since President Obama's historic election, you can follow a pattern that plays out across our nation's history: meaningful progress followed by vicious backlash; resistance and struggle that sometimes culminate in hard-fought victories for social and racial justice.

The cycle would repeat.

But sometimes even modest progress sees a backlash that stalls *any* forward momentum for years—and sometimes decades.

Consider what happened after the end of the Civil War.

For Black Americans alive at the time, the Union victory was utterly transformational for their lives: Black men and women, finally free, charted a new destiny for themselves. Since we first arrived in this country in Jamestown, Virginia, in 1619, we'd been property. Traded and sold up and down the country for centuries. Now, finally, we could farm our own land, start our own business, and earn a wage.

For the first time in American history, we ran for and *won* elected office. We did this in *the South*, of all places, where Black people represented a majority of voters for the Republican Party. In those days, the Republican Party was the "Party of Lincoln," which was widely viewed as the political champion of civil rights and Black Americans. I emphasize *the South* here because it's easy to forget that once upon a time, the South was an engine of inclusion in our democracy—a bastion of racial representation at the highest levels of our government.

Often we accept, without examination or inspection, the argument that the South is forever entrenched in its conservatism. But the reality is that, even today, there are more Black Americans and people of color in the South than in any other part of the country. Our politics reflect choices. And those choices are a function of leadership.

Anyone who chooses to lead will make better choices if we understand our history.

The period after the end of the Civil War, aptly termed *Reconstruction*, represented America's first truly great civil rights era. As the Union welcomed the seceded Southern states back into the country, the political fortunes of Black Americans dramatically changed. In the 1870s, Southern states elected *more than 2,000*

Black leaders at the state and local levels and even sent sixteen Black Americans to serve in the United States Congress.[3] Those early gains generated enormous optimism in Black communities. Many assumed we would continue to make huge economic, social, and political strides; after all, Black Americans, once granted freedom, responded to centuries of enslavement by getting involved in the political process and working cooperatively and constructively with the system to govern for *all Americans*.

And then we zagged.

The progress of the 1870s confronted a devastating backlash that consumed all levels and branches of government: contested elections, gridlock, and the eventual dismantlement of America's first great civil rights era.

The Freedmen's Bureau, which helped Black people navigate an economy that wasn't built for their freedom—supporting the newly free in acquiring property, finding employment, starting a business—was shut down. Worse yet, the federal government withdrew its military protection of the formerly enslaved, opening the door to generations of vigilantes who unleashed terror on Black people until well into the twentieth century.

Opponents of freedom didn't stop there. State legislatures set to work to pass and implement laws that limited Black freedom in every conceivable way. The hope of Reconstruction morphed into the oppressive dread of Jim Crow that rigidly enforced economic and social segregation, political disenfranchisement, and a culture of terror that tormented Black Americans in their homes and communities for nearly a century.

Today, thanks to the courageous work of the Equal Justice Initiative here in Montgomery, we have documented thousands of lynchings and hundreds of race massacres and have begun to quantify the untold number of Black lives destroyed, the Black wealth decimated, and the feeling of security and belonging that evaporated for millions of Black Americans across the decades. The culture of terror touched every part of the country: it followed Black people wherever we lived, raised our families, and built our communities.

And the 2,000 Black Americans who ascended to local, state, and federal office during Reconstruction? Well, Black representation in political office plummeted to nearly zero as states overhauled their voting laws to exclude the Black vote by any means necessary, and terror organizations like the Ku Klux Klan intimidated Black voters and elected officials to further depress their democratic participation.

Of course, Black Americans did not passively endure the decades-long backlash. We resisted. We fought back. We made our way, even as Jim Crow threatened our lives and livelihoods and degraded our dignity and self-worth. (Indeed, decades later, *that* was the rationale for the Supreme Court to unanimously decide to desegregate public facilities: "Separate but equal" impacted an individual's inherent sense of self-worth. It just made people feel less than, and that isn't right.)

Many people, including my father's family, read Jim Crow's culture of "no respect" as "no chance" and began to search elsewhere for a better life. Many in my dad's family migrated to the great industrial communities in the North: New Jersey, and New York, pursuing what Isabel Wilkerson termed the "warmth of other suns." They followed the patterns of the Great Migration, which started in the years after Reconstruction and continued until the 1950s. To stay connected, Black families wrote letters back and forth, and communities began to publish newspapers and newsletters to alert our community as to how we were faring across the country. From migration emerged a national network that laid the groundwork for the eventual modern civil rights movement.

Leaders like W. E. B Du Bois, Ida B. Wells, and the NAACP's Walter White made sure the world never lost sight of the horror and terror that dominated the American Black experience by reporting lynchings and race massacres that were unfolding unchecked across the country. The growing awareness of injustice and terror further fueled the Great Migration, with more Black Americans deciding to leave the South and pursue a better life in the North.

Indeed, my father's own father, Louis Reed, ended up in Pittsburgh to search for better-paying work and to explore a new life. My dad's mother, Eula Reed, and much of the broader family did not migrate; they continued to farm and live out of what we lovingly call the Home House. The Home House was the very place I spent weekends and summers as a kid and where many of my earliest memories of family were built. Aunt Verba's great cooking: country fried steak, ham, rabbit, collard greens, corn bread, and okra—all the staples. And, of course, the hot, homemade baked cakes that we secretly pinched as children, which she sent to me on my birthdays.

Back in the North, Black migrants navigated dense cities, dirty factories, and hostile storefronts and shopkeepers. But the cities were crowded. The waves of Black Americans fleeing the South weren't the only refugees fighting to find a new life. Black Americans new to the North sought a better, more dignified life—one that was less racist and fairer—but as my father learned at an early age, racism and discrimination aren't bound by geography. Unfortunately, Black people encounter it everywhere in this country, including and especially in the big cities of the North. Some of the ethnic enclaves and communities in New York City and Boston were as unforgiving as the most segregated parts of the Black Belt.

My dad learned this the hard way when his own father was shot and killed in Pittsburgh when my dad was just eight years old.

While the circumstances of my grandfather's killing were mysterious, the loss hit my dad hard. And it forever changed his life: he had no choice but to grow up early. From an early age he helped his family survive, and even thrive, despite the difficult conditions of rural Alabama. And on some level he internalized the idea that he would always have to fight. The world wasn't fair, but he was going to devote his life to making it a little more so.

After my grandfather's death, my dad's family kept up the farmland. After all, that was their livelihood. For me, coming from Montgomery (where my father would eventually relocate as an adult), the Black Belt was another world, a place where you could reach out and touch nature. Oftentimes my older brother, Joey, and I would leave the family farm to explore long dirt roads that cut through the surrounding countryside. We also risked getting chased by wild hogs, which was terrifying. We loved every minute. Every day there was an adventure.

It was also an isolated place. We only had family down there. I grew up vaguely aware that where my dad came from, that farm, was the proverbial "wrong side of the tracks." On the one hand, there really wasn't anything there other than the farm and family. Things stayed the same. Life was hard. And not everybody was cut out for it. Some folks, unable to escape the tedium of agriculture, fell into drink or much worse. On the other hand, my dad's people always had a pride in their work and what the farm represented to them: a start in life and how they gave their children a chance, some shot at life.

In either case, no one necessarily expected greatness from my father. He was fatherless, a second-class citizen in the rough, rural hills of Alabama with no obvious career path other than survival. Some might have conjectured that his life would end in some tragic statistic.

Fortunately, two factors made the difference: my father's determination to create a different future for himself, and changing times. Coming out of the 1950s, the civil rights movement had grown out of the Brotherhood of Sleeping Car Porters, the first labor union to admit Black Americans, into a broader movement that tapped into a larger segment of the Black and white communities: domestic workers, faith leaders, students, and committed allies. That movement established the strategies, tactics, and networks that would ultimately dismantle segregation and transform the nation.

My father worked his way through school, primarily as a janitor and doing odd jobs, earning 25 cents an hour. Semester by semester, he began to amass enough credits that a degree, a profession, and a better life for him and his family were within sight. In the decades after the 1960s, he spent his career implementing the movement's hard-won gains to prevent the cause of progress from going backward.

Professionally, my dad steered toward education. His early experiences with the public school system were formative. Some of my dad's earliest heroes were the men and women who put up their own money to start the junior high school my dad attended. The same folks who traveled for miles to collect a few used basketballs and textbooks so my dad and his friends could play sports and keep with the curriculum. The example of those men and women inspired generations and shaped the entirety of the Black experience.

Despite the headwinds, Black communities had a passion for education, and teaching was a prestigious calling. Other forces were at work, too. Black people had been excluded from most trades, vocations, and corporate environments. Teaching emerged as one of the few professional tracks available to Black people, and it represented a dignified and impactful calling. After leaving the military, my dad seized his opportunity to pursue education at Alabama State with gusto.

After school, my dad went on to lead the Alabama Education Association, one of Alabama's most powerful progressive lobbies. My dad understood that the teaching profession was full of "hidden provocateurs" who were instrumental in realizing social and racial justice.[4] The fight to desegregate schools, which culminated in the landmark *Brown v. Board of Education* decision, was perhaps *the* front line in the civil rights movement. Even after the decision, teachers, educators, and school leaders banded together to fight for funding and to make real, in Black schools in particular, equal opportunity in America.

Simultaneously, my dad also learned the tools of the law from people like Fred Gray, the civil rights attorney who led the legal challenge to desegregate Montgomery's bus system. My dad used a combination of the law and organizing to fight for equal representation, for adequate funding, and to protect the vote. Indeed, my father has often joked that his career operates from one central theme: "Every morning, I get up looking for somebody to sue."

Specifically, my dad has confronted two opponents his entire life: he calls them "Mr. Segregation" and his son, "Mr. Discrimination."

In the 1980s, when I was a young boy, I remember my dad used to give a speech in which he said, "Mr. Segregation, though he's legally dead, left a son back here called Mr. Discrimination. And the difference in the two: while Mr. Segregation wore his sheet over his suit, Mr. Discrimination wears his suit over his sheet."

My dad tangled with Mr. Discrimination and Mr. Segregation for nearly eighty years and is still at it.

My dad hasn't always been popular. For much of his career, he has been castigated as a machine politician and a troublemaker by Democrats and Republicans alike. Much ink has been spilled opining on how to beat my dad at the ballot box or in back rooms. Hell, my dad is even the central "villain" in a podcast about politics in Alabama. I think the commentariat misses the point.

Fighting for change isn't always a happy process. By its very definition, change disrupts the status quo. Achieving change threatens incumbent interests. Moreover, it's extremely challenging to fight for what's right when it's not fashionable or politically expedient. Indeed, we misremember the story of civil rights in our country. In his lifetime, Martin Luther King Jr. was profoundly unpopular. Toward the end of his life, 75 percent of Americans disapproved of Dr. King and his actions.[5] He was tireless, indefatigable in his fight for civil rights, unsatisfied with the (immense but insufficient) progress of the 1960s, and newly radicalized against the Vietnam War and the state of poverty in the United States. In other words, he never quit, and most Americans at the time couldn't stomach his fight, and his insistence, that things must change.

Why? Well, for starters, people are naturally skeptical of change. After all, most folks view change through the lens of loss. They concern themselves with what they might lose if things change rather than what they might gain. This default leads to a lot of the inertia we observe and experience in our politics. And when authentic agents of change come along, they are rarely popular. Change is hard, if necessary.

True agents of change are forged in the fires of experience. If my father mastered the mechanics of social change, it's only because his passion for a fairer democracy is rooted in lived experience. His pursuit of a more perfect union grew right out of the soil of the Alabama Black Belt where he lived through the impacts of segregation and toiled under the legacy of slavery.

Of course, the story didn't end there. My father, Joe Reed, left Evergreen, down there in Conecuh County, tough as nails and whip smart at age eighteen to enlist in the Army and fight overseas in Korea.

In the war, my father served alongside Black and white Americans alike in the recently integrated Army. When they left the country, they were strangers who were segregated and divided by the very society they were leaving to protect. On the way to basic training, white recruits would exit the bus to eat in the restaurants, leaving behind Black soldiers—who would eat whatever they could procure behind the restaurant—sitting at the back of the bus.

In war, it was something altogether different. They shared close quarters, Black and white men bunking together, missing their families together, struggling together. They risked, and many would lose, their lives for their country. In Korea—and later, in Vietnam, Iraq, and Afghanistan—they emerged as American soldiers, not white or Black soldiers. Just soldiers bonded by common cause, tragedy, and occasionally triumph.

Those young boys, Black and white, most of them poor, were changed by that experience. They learned to value one another, as Dr. King would intone on the National Mall a few short years later, not by the color of their skin but by the content of their character. But when they returned home, they discovered that while they had changed, the law had not. In 1956, just like in 1865—when Black Americans, many of them enslaved, helped a sagging Union cause finish a devastating Civil War—Black Americans were expected to shoulder America's responsibilities but not enjoy its privileges.

These men fought in Korea, but when they came home, they were excluded by the G.I. Bill. For my dad, this was a bitter pill. While his white pals from war were buying houses and starting families thanks to help from Uncle Sam, my father was starting from zero. For my dad, going back to the farm just wasn't an option.

Thankfully, there was a Black institution that represented, then and now, hope and opportunity for young men just like him: Alabama State University (ASU). Based in Montgomery, Alabama State is one of the "historically Black colleges and universities," or HBCUs. In the years immediately following the Civil War, states and the federal government, led by the Freedmen's Bureau—the federal agency set up to support formerly enslaved people after the end of slavery and the war—seeded the vast majority of HBCUs, spanning the Deep South all the way "Up South." Many of these institutions, like Alabama State, were teachers colleges, minting the very best and brightest in our community.

But fate intervened when Mr. Segregation reared his ugly head.

In those days, Montgomery's culture was reminiscent of when it was the "cradle of the Confederacy" in the early days of the Civil War. At the height of the Civil War, Montgomery was considered America's seventy-fifth-largest city but was the *second*-largest when its population of enslaved people were included in the count.

Then and now, Montgomery very much feels like a great capital city, with its Gothic architecture and clean layout. In design and beauty, Montgomery rivals the city centers one would encounter in any number of European cities. But beneath the beauty is a nasty tradition of exclusion and subjugation that extends back to the days when Montgomery led the world in importing enslaved people from along the Alabama River and via its major train depot.

Even with slavery's abolition, that *culture* of exclusion and subjugation lived on in Mr. Segregation and his son, Mr. Discrimination.

Fresh off a fight for the country, my dad, like every Black American in the country, couldn't enjoy lunch at a city lunch counter or use its restrooms.

Or hold most jobs.

Or live in most communities.

Or walk across town.

Or go to the movies.

It was too much.

My dad and a dozen other student activists started to stage sit-ins at Montgomery's courthouse lunch counter. He was student body president by then, popular and respected by his peers, and hell-bent on disrupting the status quo. They were guided by the Reverend Ralph Abernathy, Dr. King's number two and a Montgomery resident who lived just off campus near Alabama State.

They were strategic. The choice of the *courthouse* lunch counter was important. It was a public lunch counter. The fight to desegregate *private* spaces would come later and only after public spaces were won.

They paid a price for standing up for what they believed. Alabama State put my dad and the other student activists on probation, as they ran afoul of the law and the many city ordinances that insisted Black people couldn't eat sitting alongside whites.

For my dad, it was too painful to quit. All he had to do was remember when his white friends from the Army enjoyed a leisurely meal in a restaurant while he and the other Black soldiers ate out of a box on the bus. The indignity was too much. And it needed to end.

Those student activists succeeded, of course. With support from Rev. Abernathy and folks like Fred Gray who petitioned the courts, they eventually helped topple public segregation in Montgomery and set up a bigger fight for the future of the city.

As for my dad, he never looked back.

Coming home as an American GI who confronted intense discrimination from the very nation for which he risked his life was *radicalizing*. And ASU created the context in which he could constructively channel his anger and frustration. As a result, he worked with leaders whom we regard today as Civil Rights Greats: the Reverend Dr. Martin Luther King Jr., Ralph Abernathy, and Rosa Parks. Then, however, they were just Rev. King, Rev. Abernathy, and Mrs.

Parks—dedicated leaders who leaned on students like my dad and committed volunteers from the community (many of them domestic workers) to integrate lunch counters, stage protests, and execute campaigns, like the bus boycott, that flexed the economic might of the Black community, creating a cost—and pain—for those who fought to keep our world segregated and divided.

The civil rights victories of the 1960s were just the beginning. By 1975, my dad won a seat on the city council as one of Montgomery's first Black elected officials since Reconstruction. And by the early 1980s, having mastered the mechanics of legislative redistricting by redrawing those districts at the local, state, and federal levels in proportion to the Black population, he paved the way for generations of Black elected officials in Alabama—single-handedly enfranchising the state's Black political leadership, culminating in the election of Montgomery's first Black mayor in 2019. His son.

✳ ✳ ✳

Growing up, my brother and I would ride in the back of my dad's Oldsmobile most weekends as he drove across the state, meeting with local leaders, organizing, and giving speeches. We must have sat on the floor, stood in the back, or watched from behind the stage at every Black church, school, community center, neighborhood, and community association meeting in the state of Alabama.

No matter the audience, my dad delivered the same message: "All people deserve a good education and the dignity of work. It's about basic fairness and giving everyone a shot. When we finally do that, Alabama will be stronger for it." Sometimes he would drive two or three hours to give twenty minutes of remarks. That was the job. In his mind, you changed a state by winning hearts and minds, one person at a time.

He never forgot the Black Belt, either. Through his hard work, Alabama's Black Belt reemerged as the "Blue Belt" as my father educated and helped enfranchise Black voters in state and local races. His efforts mattered because he helped give people a voice in a democracy that wasn't necessarily built for them but could be changed to better serve them. Over the course of his life and mine, political representation in Alabama has looked more and more like Alabama. The avowed segregationist politics of George Wallace in the 1960s has receded, and there are more of us in public life working to improve the life of every Alabamian.

It was during those long drives that my father preached to us. At that time, most ten-year-old children might have debated with their dad about whether Willie Mays or Duke Snider was the greatest center fielder of all time. (The answer: Willie Mays, of course.) That wasn't my experience. My dad's singular priority was to teach and shape us. During those long car rides, my dad shared his code:

"Keep God in the forefront. Pray and don't be embarrassed to ask people to pray for you, because you'll need it."

"There's nothing politically right that's morally wrong."

"Give your service but never your soul."

"You want to remember that the hottest place in hell is reserved for those who maintained their neutrality in a time of moral crisis."

"Some folks say politics is dirty. Politics is a noble profession. It's 'politricks' that's dirty."

"Let your handshake be your contract and your word your bond."

"Keep in mind that you can't send for your lunch by way of a hungry boy. He'll eat it! Leaders who are hungry are greedy. They'll let their stomachs prevail over their principles."

"Watch what people do rather than listen to what they say."

"Of all crimes, the worst crime is ingratitude."

"Remember, what goes around comes around. No army is stronger than an idea whose time has come. It is better to make change afraid than to be afraid of change."

"Everything old is not bad and everything new is not good."

"Make new friends but never leave an old friend in order to make a new one. Nothing is more painful than betrayal by a person who you believed was once your friend."

He shared lessons from his days as an organizer when he took orders directly from Dr. King and Rev. Abernathy during the Montgomery campaign to integrate lunch counters. My father recalled hilarious stories about the friendships he built with people like United States Representative Jim Clyburn when they were just two young college leaders and fraternity brothers trying to start the Student Nonviolent Coordinating Committee (SNCC) in Montgomery. But my father didn't dispense wisdom for its own sake. He was teaching us. He was raising us to be strong. He saw us as future leaders, and for better or worse, he always talked to us that way.

Like the Preacher's Kid, I was "the other P.K." The Politician's Kid. When I was young, I didn't always appreciate the pearls of wisdom that I heard while sitting around in my parents' living room, or in church, or at certain community commemorations. Because civil rights leaders and their lessons were omnipresent, they were easy to take for granted. Heck, when you were small, you would just tune it out.

It wasn't until I was older, around the start of fourth grade, that I began to fully understand the importance of the lessons my dad was imparting.

One day and a specific moment marked the turning point.

It was early afternoon and I was home from school. The house was empty. My dad was at work and my mother was out running errands with my brother tagging along. My dad's personal line rang. We had two phone lines, one for the family, another for my dad's political business. As a matter of habit, I rarely answered my dad's personal line. I don't know why I did that day. Perhaps it was because I was in the fourth grade and beginning to get more engaged in my dad's work. My confidence was building and my sense of self developing. Whatever the reason, I answered the phone *that day.*

"Joe Reed's residence. May I ask who is speaking?"

"Is Joe Reed home?"

"No, he's not, can I take a message?"

Long pause.

"Tell that nigger if he doesn't shut up, I am going to blow his G—d d—m head off."

Click.

My face turned white as a sheet. A lump formed in my throat as chills ran up and down my body. My ears were ringing. I was terrified. It took several moments for me to realize I had wet myself. For the first time in my life, I was scared—truly and deeply scared.

When my father got home that evening, I tearfully shared what had happened. As I spoke to him, his eyes went dull. I could sense his sadness. His shoulders slumped. His body language suggested that he knew this was coming, as if it was only a matter of time before I found out why he kept both a public phone number and a personal line.

We sat down at the kitchen table. He somberly explained the

concepts of hate and racism. "Some people do not want the same things for everybody. They want to hold other people down because of what they look like or where they come from. That's why I do the work I do. It's also why I raise you boys to treat everybody equally and with respect."

Afterward he walked me to the garage and invited me to sit in the passenger seat of the Oldsmobile. I was confused but excited. I tentatively opened the big, heavy passenger door and climbed into the seat. My small body sank into the soft leather. My short legs dangled off the edge of the seat, not quite touching the floor. My dad reached over my lap to open the glove compartment. A gleam hit my eye as he pulled out a fully loaded .500 Smith & Wesson Magnum revolver. "I learned to keep this here after Medgar Evers was gunned down in his driveway."

That's why we never rode in the front seat. That's why my dad always parked inside the garage and closed the door before coming into the house after work.

When I asked my father why he hadn't shared any of this before, he responded, "My job is to hold a crown high above your head so you grow into it. I am raising kings. Bigotry has no place in our household. It will only hold you down and make you small. I don't want you internalizing those messages as who you are, even if others can't help but see you with hateful eyes.

"And you've got to show the world, every single day, your greatness. As our people fight for change, we will break barriers. But never forget: it's not enough to be the *first*. Always strive to be the *best*. The power of your example must shine through in everything you do."

What my dad taught me, and what I came to understand, is this: before laws change, people have to *believe* that change is possible. Breaking barriers *and* being excellent in the fight for what's right—not simply being the first in whatever it is you're doing—is the key to changing hearts and minds because it's that example that inspires others to join you in a righteous cause. That isn't always easy or necessarily fair, but it's essential to creating change.

I was lucky to grow up in a house where change was always possible. My father raised me in that Oldsmobile. He raised me on those hard truths. And he raised me to stretch myself, to rise, to never stop until I was wearing that crown.

That's not just my story. That's not just Joe Reed's story. That's *our* story. The story of Black men in America. It's my honor to have lived, and to tell, this piece of it.

✳ ✳ ✳

My name is Steven Reed. I am Montgomery, Alabama's fifty-seventh mayor and the first to be Black. Every day, I work hard to be the *best* mayor for Montgomery by working to change her trajectory and inspire her people to imagine a different future.

I am, if you can't already tell, a proud son of the "Moses Generation," the civil rights movement's Greatest Generation. That movement was propelled by national figures such as Rosa Parks, whose boycott famously ignited the modern civil rights movement by insisting that the Montgomery bus system desegregate, and Dr. King, who organized the march from Selma to Montgomery to make a national call for voting and civil rights. I was raised acutely aware of their legacy and internalized, from an early age, lessons in leadership exhibited in what they accomplished and how they lived.

And while the enemies of the movement stopped at nothing to halt racial progress in our country, the civil rights movement was bigger than the historic figures at its helm. And it certainly didn't die with Dr. King, whose spirit lives on in millions of Americans committed to bending the "moral arc of the universe" toward justice.

In the decades since the 1960s, local leaders like my father picked up the baton from the "drum major for justice" to drive the next wave of change through the 1970s, 1980s, and 1990s: the fight for representation and political enfranchisement of Americans of all races, defending the gains of the 1960s from those who would turn back the clock on progress, and finally, fulfilling Dr. King's dying vision of economic justice and opportunity for all.

Collectively, the Moses Generation led our community out of the wilderness of American apartheid. They brought us closer to the day when all people, regardless of their race, religion, gender, or creed, are treated fairly under the law and by one another. My father's generation envisioned a nation in which any child could go as far as their ambition and talent could take them. I was lucky to come of age in *that* world—from a young age, I could see so much further than what my father envisioned for himself as a young boy, growing up without a father and with no resources of his own, in Conecuh County, Alabama, decades before.

As the Bible says, Moses did not live to cross the Jordan River into the Promised Land. That opportunity, and solemn responsibility, fell instead to Joshua. I am a member of the Joshua Generation here in Montgomery, the epicenter of the civil rights movement and home to Bryan Stevenson's Equal Justice Initiative, and it is our task to bring our people to the Promised Land.

Reaching the Promised Land means winning the fight for our democracy.

It demands that we eradicate the racial wealth gap.

It requires us to end the horrors of mass incarceration and restore opportunity, dignity, and hope in our most vulnerable communities.

Above all else, reaching the Promised Land calls us to cultivate the next generation and pass down the culture, the teachings, and the value system that our forefathers and foremothers carried before us.

This is a deeply important point because on some level every generation is the Joshua Generation. There is always work to be done and a task to carry forward. The revolutionaries who started the country were challenged immediately by the abolitionists who knew we were not truly free. The abolitionists were followed by the brave soldiers of the Union Army. When the Confederates laid down their arms, America saw its first Black political leaders during the era of Reconstruction. When the backlash came, millions of Black Americans endured and stood up to the horrors of Jim Crow—the lynch mobs and domestic terrorists like the Ku Klux Klan—to build up Black families and Black communities in spite of the powerful forces trying to tear us down.

Through the world wars and a global Depression, the Joshua Generation always answered the call. They did so again when farm boys like my father returned home from another war to wage a different kind of battle here at home. A nonviolent battle that transformed the soul of the nation by delivering fundamental change, centuries in the making.

Much has been written about that generation. Less has been written about what it was like to grow up in the movement as a young person, particularly in the decades after the "golden era" of civil rights. The "golden era" of the civil rights movement is a misnomer. The movement didn't end or even reach its peak when Dr. King "had a dream." Nor did the culture wars of the 1960s give way to acceptance of all the changes generated in the years before.

Quite the contrary.

Like the Reconstruction heroes after the civil war, the Moses Generation confronted backlash in the 1970s, 1980s, and 1990s. When Ronald Reagan gave his infamous "states' rights" speech at the Neshoba County Fair in Mississippi, just miles from where the bodies of James Chaney, Andrew Goodman, and Michael Schwerner had been found sixteen years prior, he articulated the strategy of the "New Right" as they sought to gut the gains of the civil rights movement and reshape the country in their image: unfettered capitalism, the elimination of public property like schools and parks, no taxes, and the elimination of services like public housing and food stamps. What went unsaid was "dog whistled." Meanwhile, leaders like my mom and dad fought to secure the victories of the movement during those years while raising families and building communities that could stand up to the onslaught of discrimination, ignorance, and intolerance, and produce children who could hold their heads up high.

As parents, teachers, and mentors, the Moses Generation continually nurtured our collective identity. When I look back on my childhood, the signs of that nurturing are everywhere: in the T-shirts at the family reunions, the home-cooked meals after church, and the conversations—from the dinner table to the ball field to the back seat of the car.

Defending our country from the impulses of oppression is a collective struggle: it's group work. For my part, I take seriously my responsibility to pass down the lessons on leadership and manhood to the next generation—the same lessons my father learned from the civil rights greats when he was a young man fighting to change his country.

Today, I have two Black boys who are around the age I was when I received that chilling call. I have a daughter who is of college age and is part of a rising generation that is demanding change. I can see through their eyes the importance of these lessons. Young children of color confront a world that would be all too familiar to our ancestors: a democracy in crisis; a racial justice reckoning; yawning inequality, especially along lines of race; and a once-in-a-century public health crisis.

What is old is new again.

Black people, of all ages and identities, still fear for their lives: Look no further than the savage killings of Breonna Taylor, Trayvon Martin, and Ahmaud Arbery.

Our democracy and its cornerstone, the vote, are under assault.

It is existential again. And we have a responsibility to engage the next generation to fight for democracy as hard as they fight for Black lives.

Opportunity is far from universal: our schools still fail too many of our children. And the zip code in which you are born remains the strongest determinant of your success in life. The COVID-19 pandemic has only exacerbated those divides.

To meet our moment, we have work to do. It is imperative that we cultivate the next generation of Black leaders as kings and queens. The country has never been more diverse, and despite its challenges, America is today a multiracial, multicultural democracy. We have to fight to keep it that way.

Through it all, our culture and our traditions, as Black people and a community of leaders dedicated to civil rights and social justice, have seen us through. The lessons of that culture are our most important birthrights. Too often our heroes are reduced to one-dimensional caricatures or their words condensed to pithy one-liners. This does us a disservice. Whether it is Jackie Robinson or Thurgood Marshall, Wilma Rudolph or Sojourner Truth, Ruby Bridges or the Little Rock Nine, our heroes were people—fragile and fierce.

We should study them and understand their lessons.

This is especially important for Black boys and adolescents, who deserve positive affirmation designed to catalyze their hope and sense of possibility. I want to give the very same experience I received in that Oldsmobile to every young Black man coming of age, which is the opportunity to understand, through story and example, their power and potential and to acquire the knowledge to navigate a world that doesn't always root for their success.

We don't do this just for them.

We do it for us.

My father, a student at Alabama State University, was among the group of activists who integrated downtown Montgomery by sitting in at segregated lunch counters. When my father looks back on those days, he reminds whoever will listen that change often comes from those who are more willing to take risks. My dad helped changed the world *because* he was young, *because* he didn't yet have a family, *because* he didn't "know how the world works," *because* he believed things *should* change.

Youth is the engine of progress. *That's* why it's essential we pour the lessons of our ancestors into our young people.

We have a rich tradition to draw from: lessons from Black leaders that can guide us during this pivotal moment in American history. If the last decade has shown us anything, it is that the journey to the Promised Land is long and arduous. We need to do everything we can to prepare the next generation for their leg of the journey.

Chapter 2

THE MOTHERS OF THE MOVEMENT

For those who don't know me, and in part because of my dad's notoriety, I am *Joe's son*. But those who really know me understand that I am Mollie's *boy*. Throughout my entire life, to this very day, my mother, Mollie, has had an incalculable impact on me. Every pickup from practice. Every meal. Every homework assignment. She was visible and *involved* in every aspect of my life. Later, when I was starting a business and eventually a political career, she was right there as number one fan and a strategic adviser.

My mom and dad are a team. Always have been. Whether at home or in the community, they always worked as a team and rarely strayed from the same page. When it came to raising their children and fighting for civil rights, they respected each other's counsel, understood their respective strengths, and leaned on each other to endure life's challenges.

At home, though, my mom set the pace. A lifelong educator—and, in my opinion, a bit of a stickler for grammar and parts of speech—my mom held my siblings and me to high standards as we pursued our education. And she never missed an opportunity to enforce those standards. Family meals were especially important. After all, that's when my mother had a captive audience. (Nothing opens the ears more than an empty stomach. You'll agree to anything if it means getting through grace and on to eating.)

The way my mother saw it, breakfast and dinner offered a chance to align expectations. To establish and communicate priorities. To give—and receive—feedback as she listened to understand the specific contours of our lives: what was going well and what wasn't.

If that all sounds serious, well, it *was*. My parents ran a tight ship. They had to. To raise three children and work in partnership to support my dad's demanding career, my mother had to maximize every touchpoint. And if you think about it, family meals represented one of the few times we were all together.

Over breakfast early in the morning, we would pass plates of hot grits, scrambled eggs, and, if it was the weekend, bacon with biscuits and jelly as Motown hits played gently on the radio. Another staple: evening meals revolved around whatever vegetables were in season. Collard greens, string beans, squash, or peas dominated our meals, depending on the season. Early in the morning, and most evenings, our family joined together at the kitchen table to eat. As the youngest child of three, that ritual was all I ever knew as a child: me; my brother, Joey; my sister, Irva; and my mom and dad.

Mealtime wasn't just about character instruction or catching up on school. Important history lessons revolved around food. Having grown up on the farm, my mother understood where our food came from, its importance to Black culture, and its larger relevance in the American economy. Black-eyed peas, also known as field peas or cowpeas, depending on where you are, came from the motherland. As did okra, butter beans, and rice. Many Southern economies were virtually nonexistent until these crops, and the Black people enslaved to cultivate them, arrived in America. Rice and cotton played an outsized role in globalizing the Southern economy while creating enormous wealth for the white families who owned the means of production.

Traditions and rituals around food grounded our family. Black-eyed peas, as a blessing for prosperity in the home, to ring in the new year. An appreciation of the meats you turn your nose up to as a kid—chitlins (google it), pig's feet and ears, oxtails—as staples because our ancestors couldn't afford to waste *any* precious protein. In those days the good cuts of meat went only to white people. Black families still cook and serve those parts of the animal in part as a reminder of what our people endured and the creativity they employed to do so. They're good eats, too.

My mom was devoted to us kids. In ways big and small, that devotion was always present. When my mom passed a mouthwatering tin of buttered biscuits to one of the children first, my dad would almost always joke, "Come mealtime, I used to be Mr. Captain until Irva came along. Then I lost the first seat. Then I was in the second seat until Joey arrived. And then Stevie followed. Now I am back here sitting in the fourth seat, waiting on *my* biscuit."

My dad teased but the truth is my parents were a phenomenal team. They worked closely together to raise us. My dad provided us with experiences and an earful: he drove us around the city and state of Alabama to bring us into *his world*. To show us what it meant to be in community. To advocate for social justice. How to bend a system toward justice. Through my dad, I came to know Alabama—her flaws and foibles, her breadth and beauty. My dad was and still is highly relational. Through him, I met heroes of the civil rights movement and had a chance to learn from them, too.

My mom's presence, on the other hand, was quieter but no less forceful. She was the steadying force. From my mother I learned the importance of choices and follow-through. My mother exemplified a commitment to a process: showing up every day and making choices that reflected the ethos of a leader.

My dad was gone a lot for work. With breakfast, lunch, and dinner, my mom was the constant. She took us to practice. She was at all the games. She picked us up. She dropped us off. She worked her career, never taking a sick day. She taught us that our example mattered, that others were always paying attention to our choices.

Later, after my older brother and sister moved out of my parents' home, leaving just me, a young teenager, in the house, my siblings loved to suggest that I was "spoiled." To some extent, they were right. One kid in the house instead of three meant more of everything for me. (I won't deny that I helped myself to extra helpings of ice cream in those years.) But I always reminded them that I had our parents' undivided attention: our parents' four eyes were on me. Whether it was something to do with school, girls, or curfew, there was more conversation, more discipline, and more accountability.

As a former classroom English teacher and an administrator at Alabama State University, my mom vigilantly upheld expectations: she didn't take any mess.

"Steven," she asked over breakfast and again at dinner, "did you get your homework done?" The answer, of course, was "No." Nevertheless, I was always quick to offer an excuse. A few words in, she'd cut me off: "There you go again, Steven, talking your way out of trouble so fast that you talk your way right back in. There's no substitute for showing up and doing the work."

Mom knew what was up. She was too engaged not to. She was at every PTA meeting and parent-teacher conference, which wasn't good. She knew all my teachers—Ms. Smith, Mrs. Washington, Mr. Jackson, and Ms. Williams—on a first-name basis, which also wasn't good. She would cultivate them, too, as her sources of intelligence on her youngest son, which was worse.

When it came to ascertaining vital information about my performance in school, my mom had her routine. I couldn't evade her prying for long. She would call my teacher before asking innocently for a meeting. She would bring in a plate of freshly baked cookies to give as a gift, to soften them up. She'd start each meeting with a barrage of compliments: "Oh, Ms. Smith, I just love your dress. And your classroom looks spectacular. How on earth do you keep all these children in line?"

It worked every time. Hook, line, and sinker. Buttered up, just like those biscuits, my teachers spilled the tea: every cut class, talking out of turn, paper airplane contests—it all came out. And my mom always played it straight: she never let on that she expected to find it all out. "Oh, Steven did what?"—surprised but *not surprised*. The more they shared, the more leverage she had at home.

Inevitably, after every parent-teacher conference, I knew that whatever plans I *might have* had were over. "Steven, you'll never believe what I learned from Ms. Smith today," my mom would start flatly. "It's time to get the books out, buster."

My mom pushed all of us to do well in school, but she really pushed me. I think she knew intuitively that I needed the accountability—especially when I was young. Like my dad, I could talk. And I was smart. But without structure and vigilance from my mom, I wouldn't apply myself in school. I wasn't wired for it, I suppose. As a young person, I was easily distracted and *always* in a hurry: to see my friends, to jump on my bike, to play ball—to do anything, really, but schoolwork and homework. *That* was tedious, and it was hard for me to settle down and focus. I had a lot of energy that needed to go *somewhere.*

And I was a talker, too. I was perceptive. I read people and situations well. And usually I couldn't wait to tell someone about something I picked up on or observed. My mouth ran nonstop, a trait I inherited from my dad. I guess we've always had a lot to say.

My mom was undeterred. She hammered discipline into me. All those years on the farm had steeled her work ethic, and she refused to let me grow up without challenging me to forge one for myself, too. My mom quite literally made me redo every single homework assignment until I was in middle school.

When my handwriting was terrible, my mom insisted I improve it. For her, good handwriting was about professionalism and taking pride in one's work. She read every assignment I produced, and when she couldn't read my handwriting, which was often, it had to be done again. She didn't care if it was late, or if I was tired, or if I simply didn't want to do it. None of that mattered. If the work product was unacceptable, it was unacceptable. I'd either redo my homework on the spot or she would wake me early to do it again before school. Either way, it got done and it got done right.

That taught me a valuable lesson: Get it right the first time and don't cut corners. Make good choices. Every day. Show up. Follow through.

My dad reinforced my mother's lessons around work and a work ethic. He would take a core principle that my mom drilled into me, day after day, like "Don't cut corners" or "Get it right the first time," and extrapolate a broader leadership lesson.

He'd say something like "You know, your mom's right about your homework. I know it was early to get up this morning to do it all again but remember: too many people want to be crown wearers, but too few want to be cross bearers."

The implication was clear: we put our studies and communities first. And we do right by them. Sure, my parents wanted us to have a good time as children growing up, but first things were always first: our studies, helping others, our practice of faith.

It could be hard to swallow if my parents hadn't modeled those values in their own lives. Through them, I learned that "first, best" is not just about the mantle of manhood or that of leadership. It's not only about an expectation of excellence, of greatness. Fundamentally, it's about responsibility and preparation. It's about *service* and the rigors that accompany helping others. Kings don't just assume the mantle; when they do so, they are prepared to serve.

In the end, leaders are responsible for those they lead. Effective leadership begins with a willingness to bear the cross. To pay the price of leadership. Good leaders carry the weight of their decisions—all of them: the good ones, the bad ones, and the ones where it's just not clear which way it'll break.

There's a cost to bearing the cross. No doubt. My parents and their generation lived with tension and trauma. And it was constant. Nevertheless, they marched on, carrying the burdens of an entire movement on their shoulders.

We acknowledge their sacrifice, but if we're honest, we mostly celebrate the men of the movement: Dr. King, Malcolm X, Medgar Evers. Those men were great. They gave their lives. Their stories are important. Their examples are formidable. We rightly focus on all that we can learn from their lives: their successes and their failures, professional and personal.

But in our telling of history, we severely neglect the mothers of the movement—and we do so at our peril. My most important leadership lessons came through women like my mother, Mollie Perry, who *grew up in the same community as Coretta Scott King.* Who *also* played a vital role advancing civil rights, marching, boycotting, and sitting in right alongside the men of the movement.

But *after* the march, *after* church, *after* the protest, it was the women of the movement who cooked the massive feasts to feed the nonviolent army. It was the women who tended to the household, despite the demands of the movement, raising families, and caring for aging parents. While the men hung out most cool evenings after a hot, exhausting day to play pool and blow off steam by cracking jokes and trading stories, the women of the movement were laying the groundwork for the next day, the next week, the next month—working the phones to make sure the next action or campaign was set up for success.

It was tireless and, for them, utterly tiresome. For too many Black women today, not much has changed. Black women earn far less for the same work and experience a disproportionate share of bias and discrimination as they navigate the systems that govern our lives: the world of work, health care, and education. At work, Black women are often overlooked for that promotion or raise—or passed over for the job altogether. Black women experience inferior results in health care: higher infant mortality, shorter lives, and higher morbidity. And even though Black women are among the most educated segment of Americans, they pursue their education with the least amount of financial and social support.

Black women carry more responsibility, too. They are more likely to serve as head of household than white women and live in communities and neighborhoods that are less secure, less affluent, and more segregated.[1]

Despite these challenges, Black women—as activists, role models, parents, and community leaders—have played an essential role in building and extending a culture of leadership in the fight for civil rights. That contribution has been largely overlooked as the bias and discrimination Black women experience in our world has extended to our telling of history, too. In her excellent book *The Three Mothers*, Anna Malaika Tubbs uplifts the mothers of the civil rights movement and the many ways they prepared their children to navigate a society that denied their humanity from the start. The mothers of Dr. King, Malcolm X, and James Baldwin—Alberta, Louise, and Berdis— drilled into their sons both a value system and a set of leadership tools that would later prove decisive in their careers. We rarely remember these women and the countless others just like them who chose to "bear the cross" over "wearing the crown."

They exemplify selflessness, and our society is just beginning to acknowledge their sacrifice.

It is critically important to me, as the mayor of Montgomery, to uplift Black women's contributions to the movement. We write history every day, and every day we have a choice about who to celebrate and acknowledge. As a student of history and a son of the South, I *know* how important Black women are to our fight for justice. And I appreciate how important it is that we acknowledge their role: it's how we encourage and inspire the next generation. As a father, how can I expect great things from my daughter if she doesn't have examples to look to and models to follow?

We don't have a shortage of sheroes, but we need to do a better job of telling their stories. We recently dedicated a statue to Rosa Parks in commemoration of the sixty-sixth anniversary of the

Montgomery bus boycott, which many regard as the beginning of the civil rights movement. It's the event that brought Dr. King to the forefront of the movement and set in motion the powerful events that culminated in world-changing legislation just a few years later.

However, the events that led to the Montgomery bus boycott that began the first Monday of December 1955 were in motion years before the arrest of Mrs. Parks. The Women's Political Council, a group of Black professionals founded in 1946, had already focused their attention on ending the Jim Crow practices of the Montgomery city buses, which demeaned Black people (having them pay at the front of the bus before entering from the rear, for instance, or decreeing that Black people had to stand over empty seats instead of being allowed to sit down) and excluded Black communities (instead of stopping at every street corner as they did in white communities, the bus was scarce in Black communities).

The Women's Political Council outlined their proposed changes to then mayor W. A. Gayle. Although they were organized and clear in their communication, the mayor didn't act. The Women's Political Council was prepared to escalate. The council president, Jo Ann Robinson, reiterated their request in a letter to the mayor and conveyed that at least twenty-five local organizations would soon boycott the buses. The mayor still failed to act, so Black women started to resist.

The first turning point occurred when fifteen-year-old Claudette Colvin refused to give up her seat to a white woman some nine months before Rosa Parks refused to give up her seat. Ms. Colvin was a student at the segregated Booker T. Washington High School. She was also pregnant. Ms. Colvin's stance was important. She was one of the five plaintiffs that Fred Gray mobilized in his lawsuit, *Browder v. Gayle*, that eventually ended segregation on buses altogether by decree of the Supreme Court—an absolutely landmark decision.

What's important to recognize is that Ms. Colvin was the first to courageously resist when she refused to give up her seat *and* her role in the movement was intentionally obscured by its leaders at the time and, therefore, her role in history has been virtually ignored altogether. As a pregnant underage Black girl, her profile was considered too "complex" to serve as the face of the movement. Movement leaders believed her to be too young, too pregnant, and too unwed to marshal an effective public relations campaign that would generate sympathy for the cause, across racial lines. Rosa Parks, an older adult with a job and middle-class sensibilities, better fit the bill.

Undoubtedly, this must have been difficult to accept. Yet Ms. Colvin was a team player. She didn't court the press to highlight her unfair treatment; instead, she quietly supported the movement's strategy. In partnership with Fred Gray, she ignited the lawsuit that eventually ended bus segregation while Rosa Parks and others built the massive public relations campaign that would go on to shine a light on the injustice of segregation across the nation and the world.

Mrs. Parks has been celebrated worldwide and is heavily commemorated here in Montgomery.

Likely, you've never heard of Ms. Colvin.

On one level, Ms. Colvin's story is painful because she paid a high price for her sacrifice. Just two years after refusing to give up her seat, she fled Montgomery because she couldn't find work or peace in a city where she had played such a powerful role disrupting the status quo. Her criminal record followed her until 2021, when her arrest for not giving up her seat was expunged. On another level, her story is critical to share so young people can learn from it. Ms. Colvin was truly a leader. She bore the cross. She paid the price of leadership.

There are, no doubt, thousands of women like Ms. Colvin who

have played a thankless role in changing things. Indeed, historians today attribute the success of the Montgomery bus boycott to the nameless cooks, maids, and domestic workers who walked countless miles for a year to bring the city to its knees. Once in motion, more than 90 percent of Black riders on the buses participated in the boycott. Undoubtedly, many if not most of those individuals had more in common with Ms. Colvin than other movement leaders, who tended to be more educated and have greater economic means.

As we evaluate leaders and leadership and pass lessons down to the next generation, it's critical that we acknowledge the sexism and gender inequity that have characterized many social movements throughout history, including the civil rights movement. Women are more likely to bear the cross, while men, more times than not, scramble to wear the crown.

There's nothing wrong with ambition. Like any good father, I encourage my boys to step up into leadership roles and to use their voices for the greater good. I want to raise strong, good men who are unafraid to lead. However, I also encourage my boys to know when it's okay—indeed, when it's appropriate—to step aside and to champion another person's cause. Sometimes the best leaders follow, and effective leaders understand the bigger dynamics at work: the facts of someone's race, gender, or sexual orientation all play a part in how they're perceived and how their leadership is received and experienced. Without a doubt, our inability to account for those dynamics can perpetuate the very inequity we strive to eliminate.

The bottom line is this: Ms. Colvin is an American hero. Her story should have been celebrated during the civil rights movement. Today, we can learn in equal measure from her quiet, selfless leadership—the "bearing of the cross"—as well as the failure of good people and wildly effective leaders to appreciate her contribution. None of us is perfect. Learning from the civil rights movement doesn't mean accepting their leadership—and leadership decisions—uncritically. After all, the most important trait of any leader is to take responsibility for one's decisions—the good, the bad, and the ones when you don't know which way it'll break.

✴ ✴ ✴

My mother's people hail from Perry County, Marion, Alabama, which is just outside of Selma and ninety miles west of Montgomery.

Like my father's family, my mother's people farmed the Alabama Black Belt. They, too, toiled under the torment of Mr. Segregation.

As children, we called my mom's parents, David and Lela Perry, Big Daddy and Mother Dear, terms connoting endearment and profound respect. We revered my mother's parents. They were the constant, affirming presence in my early childhood.

I remember my granddad, Big Daddy. He was a tall, thin man with sun-browned skin from his decades of working the farm. He was kind and quiet. Day in, day out, he did his duty: working the farm, looking after Mother Dear, attending church, and playing with us children.

And I absolutely loved Mother Dear. She spoiled me. Honestly, she let me do just about anything. When my mother wouldn't let me have something—a slice of freshly baked pecan or sweet potato pie, for instance—as soon as I walked into Mother Dear's house, she would let me have it.

Their hugs were big, too. Full of love. It's hard to put into words, but they gave the kind of hugs that made you feel completely safe and accepted. It's funny: Big Daddy and Mother Dear didn't have much, but in retrospect they had everything. They had each other and they had so much love—for us, for my parents, for anyone who walked through that front door.

When I was growing up, you would be hard-pressed to find my

dad back on the farm. He certainly didn't look down on agricultural work, but he didn't go out of his way to do any of it, either. He'd had his fill. My mom, on the other hand, really *knew* how to plant and how to pick: she maneuvered rows of corn, okra, and green beans with a speed and a grace that was mesmerizing. When we visited Big Daddy and Mother Dear, it was never long before my mom was out in the field, helping them tend to whatever needed tending without saying a word. That kind of care and commitment is in her DNA.

When my mother came of age, she left to attend Alabama State, leaving behind Big Daddy and Mother Dear, along with the family farm. Like my dad, my mom also aspired to a career in education. After graduation, she started working at Alabama State, where she built a career and a legacy. Through the decades, she's touched thousands of lives, shaping and molding Black men and women during the critical years when they come of age.

Part of her legacy shows up in my own education, which started on the campus of ASU at the Zelia Stephens Early Childhood Center. Named after an educator in Montgomery, the early childhood center brought children from all walks of life to the campus for instruction.

It worked so well for our family. My mom always picked me up and dropped me off. The center gave me a great start in life. It had a vibrant culture that conveyed a high level of expectation to every child. And it was, for the most part, all Black. I'm still friends to this day with some of the people I met at Zelia Stephens. Many went on to advance the cause of education in their careers. One of them, Fred Brock, co-founded Valiant Cross Academy, which develops leaders by providing a loving, stable educational environment for young men. I've known Fred for forty years. That's the power of Zelia Stephens.

In retrospect, I marvel at how effectively my mother balanced it all—no, juggled it. She raised three children and was a vocal and active partner in my father's work, all while building a righteous legacy at Alabama State as a professional educator. Like so many Black women, my mother simply set about her work at home and in the community, never really putting herself ahead of anyone else. She lived a life of service and sacrifice.

And the system—and structure—worked for my mother. Through Zelia Stephens, my mom effectively had childcare available to her at ASU. She also had an employer that understood the value of flexibility for working parents, especially working women, as they also carry the family burden. That system and structure valued my mother and her contribution and helped her pursue a career while she raised a family. Laws and public investments that expand access to childcare and ensure that women are paid fairly and equally for their work go a long way in sustaining the critical contributions women, and especially Black women, make across our society.

It also helped that my father valued and respected my mother's role. I can't exactly pinpoint what made my father different from other men in his generation in this regard—maybe it was the fact that he had lost his dad so early in life and his own mother was the head of household, the sole provider—but my dad didn't engage in a lot of the misogyny that, candidly, characterized part of the civil rights movement.

Perhaps my dad always felt a little bit like an outsider in the movement, too. After all, he grew up poor and relatively isolated compared to other leaders in the movement, many of whom were raised middle class or even upper-middle class. My dad always felt the class divide in the civil rights movement. His mannerisms and way of speaking can be folksy, almost simple, which belies a fierce intelligence. Also, he didn't have the "pedigree" relative to a lot of the senior leaders of the movement, which led some to underestimate him. Whatever the reason, my dad also regarded my mother and the women of the movement with reverence and respect. I suspect, on some level, he had empathy for their position.

There is so much to learn from the great civil rights generation. There's a lot to criticize, too. Black women like my mother made the movement work. Nevertheless, they endured a casual, pervasive sexism as they made those contributions. Since then, Black women have received a fraction of the credit they deserve in the history books. The good news is that it's never too late to rectify that wrong. Recognition and credit cost us nothing, and they are so, so important. The urgent news is that we must immediately begin that work. The next generation requires it.

Thanks to my mother, church also played a significant role in my upbringing. While we didn't go to church every night as many did, we were there dutifully every Sunday. And every Sunday young people were expected to give the Sunday school report. My mother insisted we take seriously our preparation for the report because the entire community was paying attention. I invested hours of preparation during the weeks when it was my turn. To give the report, I stood before the entire congregation, dressed in my best suit and tie, before walking through a structured set of remarks that responded to our study and reflection in Sunday school.

When giving the report, there was nowhere to hide. If you had nerves, you learned to conquer them. A shaky voice and a painful lump in your throat didn't serve you—it was embarrassing to choke on your remarks—so I learned to control my breathing. I discovered a practice akin to meditation. I would take deep breaths in as I silently, slowly counted *One...two...three...four...five... six...* and so on, until my heart rate slowed and I found the strength in my voice.

I also learned that I did the best when I spoke on topics that resonated with me—*that were authentic.* For me, at least, to speak on anything else was to phone it in. I particularly loved the parables that mirrored, in some roundabout way, struggles in my own life. David and Goliath for when I was dealing with a bully at the local YMCA. Jonah and the whale for when I was doing—and redoing—all that homework. The book of Job for when I felt tempted to do anything and everything *except* the right thing.

The coolest thing about church was that it was truly a melting pot, bringing together teachers and educators, doctors and lawyers, tradesmen, stay-at-home parents, community leaders. *Everyone.* I think about people like Juan Ford, an educator and pastor, who went on to impact young people in another community. I trace a lot of their success as leaders, public speakers, and thinkers back to that small congregational church and the report. We were lucky: it was an engaged congregation. If we needed work on something, they'd help us. They wouldn't let us split our infinitives for long. And they always encouraged us.

Of course, education was emphasized in the home, too. Our household maintained an ethos of Serious Education. How could it not? Both of my parents were career educators. Education was their path out of the poverty and toil of the Black Belt. It was the deciding factor in my parents' life trajectory, and they were intent on educating me and my siblings in a way that set us up for success.

They were serious: no television on school nights; we almost always had homework, even when we didn't; and every interaction with our parents tied back to some lesson or takeaway. They were always teaching us.

Because I was the youngest of three, my relationship to education was more complicated than my older siblings'. My brother and sister were dedicated, serious students. Although my brother played baseball, and my sister cheered, academics always came first.

For me, it was a bit different. I *loved* sports—watching them, talking about them, thinking about them, debating them, playing them. Through sports, I finally had a place for all my energy. And sports were a unifier in my social life. They are how I bonded with people of all ages, races, and class backgrounds. They gave us heroes to emulate, football greats like Walter Payton, Mel Blount, and Tony Dorsett, and basketball legends like Dr. J, Magic, Michael Jordan, and Larry Bird. I can't tell you how many hours I spent debating my uncles and cousins about who the best boxer of all time was, folks like Joe Louis, Muhammad Ali, Joe Frazier, Sugar Ray Leonard, and others.

Even my parents got it. Usually, there was no TV in the house unless *Wide World of Sports* was on. That was the exception. In retrospect, their tacit approval underscored the important role sports played in our lives.

Sports weren't all fun and games, though. It was a battlefield, too. I was a smaller kid, always near the end of the class in weight and height. Looking back, my dad's prominence in the community also invited some degree of trouble. The combination of having a bit of notoriety because of who my parents were and being a bit smaller led other kids to pick on me. In turn, I developed a bit of a chip on my shoulder.

The socioeconomic diversity of church carried over into the community in which I grew up and the schools I attended. I didn't grow up in a gated community. I didn't grow up in a posh planned subdivision or urban development. My community and the public schools I attended pulled from all levels of socioeconomic status. Many of the kids in my neighborhood had it tough. And that toughness, and the conflict around our diversity, played out in sports. A loss in football could lead to a fight. A foul on the basketball court could turn into a fight. A hard tackle was almost *always* a fight. In contrast, when I reflect on children today, I see that we put so many pads around kids that they don't always know how to respond to conflict or a setback.

As a smaller kid with a prominent dad, I attracted my fair share of conflict. As a result, I learned to never back down from a fight. Today, we would call some of it, particularly in elementary school, roughhousing. But occasionally, it veered into the territory of bullying. Back then, in either case, *it was just life*. It was such a commonplace occurrence that after a few years I developed the tools to confront conflict head-on. I learned to navigate a social group that was as diverse as it was complex. Through the years, I've spoken to a lot of youth groups as well as parents, and invariably the topic of conflict comes up. My bottom line is this: if somebody tells you that they haven't ever lost a fight, then they have never fought anyone their size. Because you're going to lose some fights. That's just the reality.

I remember fighting my friend Xavier. We were good friends, but occasionally we would butt heads, as good friends occasionally do. I can't remember what we were fighting about, but we were in the third grade at the time, and I clearly remember that as I was getting ready to swing a punch, Xavier karate kicked me in the stomach.

When the sole of his foot connected with my insides, it felt like I had been hit by a car, and in that moment I thought—no, I *believed*—I was going to die. Bruce Lee was a huge star back then, and there was a Black actor named Jim Kelly who starred alongside him in his most popular film, *Enter the Dragon*. Jim Kelly's character, Mr. Williams, was tall, handsome, and strong, and he had a fearsome side kick. Well, apparently, Xavier had been studying Mr. Williams, because that day he knocked the wind out of me. I laugh about it to this day.

Chapter 3

THE PAIN OF CHANGE

My parents, especially my mom, encouraged me to build relationships across lines of difference—"to understand before seeking to be understood"—so that I could model better behaviors than the ones my parents encountered in the deeply segregated world of the 1940s and '50s.

As such, diversity defined my childhood. Busing pulled students, Black and white alike, from neighborhoods at all income levels. Many of my Black peers grew up in public housing. I learned to interact with kids from all walks of life.

Socially, I was a success. But my grades weren't very good. Especially my conduct grades. In school, I couldn't seem to do anything right. My report cards from those years—and my mom still has these, by the way—indicated that I failed to follow instructions and I couldn't stop talking in class.

Ouch.

"Steven, until your conduct grades improve, we're going to pull you out of football," my mom said matter-of-factly one evening over dinner. I was halfway through a fistful of corn bread and nearly choked on it as I processed the words tumbling out of her mouth. "You're a leader on the field but you're not a leader off the field. That's not how it works. If you turn it around, maybe you can play next season," my mother continued, her voice brighter and more hopeful. I wasn't buying it. My plate, piled high with collard greens and ham, suddenly looked a lot less appetizing.

This was a reckoning. My conduct grades had slipped long enough. I knew she was serious. My mother loved me. She was and is, to this day, my number one fan. But she didn't take any mess.

I was in a tough position. No matter how engaging I found a class or how compelling I found a teacher, I couldn't wait until the bell rang in the last period and it was *finally* time to suit up, put on our pads, and hit the field. Sports were always my first love. And let's be fair: good conduct was in the eye of the beholder. What my teachers saw as troublemaking behavior I regarded as inspired and free-spirited.

Besides, I absolutely *loved* football. Everything about it. The intensity and the action. The strategy and tactics. *The hitting*.

But my mom's words were the ultimate gut punch. It hurt worse than Xavier's karate kick.

When I protested her decree, she cut me off. "Steven, you need to learn one lesson and one lesson clearly, you hear me? *When the pain you're in is greater than the pain of change, you'll change.*"

"The pain of change," I thought to myself. *What the hell does that mean?*

Well, I found out. Instead of football practice, I had chores. And lots of them. They were never-ending. Take out the trash. Do the dishes. Organize the garage. Pull weeds out of the garden. Mow the lawn. Wash the house siding. Vacuum the rugs. Sweep the floors. *Go pull more weeds*. It was insanity. And I was miserable.

I moped and groaned around the house. I made a real display of my displeasure. I even contemplated civil disobedience. But my dad cut that off at the root. "Don't even think about it, Steven. Take the damn trash out," he said curtly when I attempted my one and only failed protest.

This stretched on for what felt like weeks but in reality was days. And mercifully, God had plans other than weeds for me. While he always works in mysterious ways, this time his divinity showed up by way of my brother, Joe.

First, a bit about Joe. We were as thick as thieves growing up— we'd spent too many hours together in the Oldsmobile not to be— but the truth is we were different from each another. Joe, as the older son, was named after my dad. As the namesake, he had less margin for error. That pressure influenced his personality. At school and at home, he never colored outside the lines; his homework was always done and his chores completed. He was dutiful. I guess that's why he eventually became a lawyer. Years later, when a group of community leaders approached me about running for probate judge, an important elected position here in Alabama, I assumed they had confused me with Joe. In my mind, then, he was the more obvious candidate for the political path my dad followed.

As kids, Joe was more naturally a risk-taker. Joe was also more of a jokester at home. I think the weight of expectation, resulting from being my father's oldest and namesake, represented an uneasy burden for him. Joe was the first to lighten the mood when things got too heavy: he was the first to crack a joke after the minister delivered a serious sermon. Those knuckles were rapped a few times.

Joe was always ready to horse around when our cousins or kids from the neighborhood came over to the house. He'd jump on your back or steal the ball when you were practicing your free throws. Through it all, Joe knew how to walk the line—good at school and a ton of fun to be around.

But because he was the oldest son, when he did slip up, he paid a swift and heavy price. It was almost as if my parents, educators straight out of the Old Testament, needed to make an example out of Joe so that I stayed in line.

When Joe's grades slipped, my mother took away football. It hurt. Joe watched from the sidelines all year. It was painful for him, and I am not sure he ever regained his enthusiasm for the sport after that. He moved on to other things.

But this night, as my head hung low, my face barely above the plate as I contemplated my fate, it was Joe who spoke up.

"You know, Mom, Steven might be more motivated to improve his grades if he stays in football," he offered. His tone was thoughtful and considered.

"And why is that?" my mother fired back.

"Well, I just remember when you and dad pulled me out of

football. My grades didn't get any better, at least not right away. I just stopped playing football."

Damn good point. *Touchdown.*

My mother studied Joe's face. They locked eyes. My eyes darted back and forth between them. *Don't break eye contact; hold your ground,* I prayed quietly, half to Joe, half to God.

"Okay," my mother said finally. "Steven can stay in football, but if his grades don't improve by the second half of the season, football is over, no questions asked."

Joe smiled and gave me a knowing look: *I got you.*

That night I felt especially lucky to call Joe my brother. Joe was onto something, too. Sometimes, when you're trying to motivate someone, punishment—at least as a preemptive measure—doesn't always work. It can have the opposite effect. It can demotivate.

That doesn't mean eliminating accountability altogether. Joe and my parents helped me understand the stakes of my decisions. I loved sports—everyone knew that—but life wasn't all about sports. There were more important things to consider, and at that age those things included school, my grades, and ultimately my future. My parents knew I was unfocused in school, and while I always did well enough to get a B, they knew I was capable of more. I showed it, too, at least occasionally. I was a natural leader. I would win student government elections, and my peers would ask me to lead specific student groups, but I struggled to sustain my interests there.

Honestly, I think part of it was that it came a little too easily for me. I needed a challenge to stay stimulated. Because I was a smaller kid, sports were harder for me, and I felt like I had something to prove. Besides, I *really loved football.*

Joey bought me some time to turn it around at school, and I did—at least, for the most part. I always walked the line—I was and remain a bit of a contrarian, and there's nothing like an authority figure to bring out my rebellious side. But I honored my mother's wishes and stepped it up at school. I also put more time and effort into sports.

✳ ✳ ✳

It's true my grades weren't great, especially when I was younger. But, looking back, it's equally true that many of my teachers weren't big fans of my dad, and I paid the price as a result. My dad led the most powerful political organization in the state, and one of the most influential teacher organizations in the country. He also made a lot of controversial decisions, including the choice to merge an all-white and an all-Black education association into one. The merger was the right call: it made the progressive cause for education an issue around which everyone could rally, no matter their race. But the merger didn't do anything to reduce the inherent suspicion Black and white educators carried toward one another. After the merger, if a white educator was promoted to principal of a mostly Black school, there would be an uproar. The same thing would happen if a Black educator advanced in a mostly white school. Race was *the* dividing line, and despite the fact that progressive educators were better advocating with one voice, my dad's decision to merge the associations created a lot of enemies for him—and for me.

By the time I was in the fourth grade, it was clear that I needed to go to another school. I just couldn't get along with my teachers, and it was beginning to take a serious toll on my personality. My mother was worried that as I grew older I would dig in and begin to resist her commands to redo homework or study over the weekend. It wasn't only that I was a hyper kid; I didn't like all my teachers because I was being treated unfairly. By tanking my schoolwork, I was resisting their bullying.

My mom picked up on all of it and had me bused out to Vaughn Road, where I spent the fourth, fifth, and sixth grades. Vaughn

Road was a newer school in a better-developed, revitalized part of the city. The kids who walked to that school were mostly white.

When I first showed up at Vaughn Road, I knew I was in for a change because it was *different*. Vaughn Road was a majority white school that was solidly middle if not upper-middle class. Military families stationed at the nearby Maxwell Air Force Base made up a lot of the surrounding community.

For those of us who were bused in, just getting to school required adjustment because the route was longer. I saw more neighborhoods across the city. I sat next to kids from both public housing projects and more affluent communities. I went from a tight-knit community school where most of the students were Black and had grown up together to a school that reflected the full diversity of Montgomery. That occasionally contributed to tensions: two students from different communities might get into a fight at the bus stop or even on the bus, but the ride was so long that inevitably they'd have to sit together uncomfortably until they made it to school. At the time, it was a bit of an experiment for communities of different races and income levels to send their children to the same school.

This was an interesting time from a youth development perspective as well. These were the years in which girls matured earlier than boys, and for the first time in my life girls emerged as a strong presence. And not in the ways you might think. The girls at Vaughn Road were tough. Hell, some even put you in a headlock. Those girls weren't playing, and whether they were white or Black, they sent a message to the boys: Don't mess with us. They were smart, too, and active in student leadership. I remember feeling a little intimidated by the impressive and, at the time, towering girls in my class.

In time, I learned to talk to Black girls, but it took a while. Unlike elementary school, you can't just write one a note saying, "Do you like me? Check yes or no." That ain't flying no more. Now you've got to have some game. You've got to be able to talk and know what's cool and what's not, who's in fashion and who is out. Heck, even how you danced changed from year to year. What might have worked in the sixth grade would spell doom for your chances on the dance floor in the seventh.

Intimidation was an early theme when I first arrived at Vaughn Road. I lost a little bit of status—and stature—in the transition. In the neighborhood school that I had left behind, I was a good athlete, popular, and a student leader, even though I was a smaller kid. At Vaughn Road, they pulled from a larger set of communities: the good students were smarter, the good athletes were better, and the student leaders were more sophisticated. They had to be. Serving as a hall monitor (a tricky job in which you basically rat out your friends) or on the student council in a school with both Black *and* white kids was just harder. If I was going to be successful, I quickly realized that I needed to improve as a student and, more importantly, develop as a person; otherwise, I risked getting left behind.

I got off to a bumpy start at Vaughn Road when I failed the test for the gifted and talented program. You would think that would be the nail in the coffin of my education. Fortunately, the culture of the school wasn't competitive but nurturing. A support system surrounded me after that early setback, and it wasn't long before I settled into my new school and saw my grades improve. Sure, the kids were smart and a lot of them performed better than I did, at least at first. But the teachers, the counselors, and even the other students encouraged us.

There were more resources, too. Better libraries, tutors, and mentors. This might sound inconsequential, but everything was better *lit*—the cafeteria, the classrooms, the hallways. It was easier to see the assignment on your desk. I didn't have to squint as much to make out the words on the page. Just seeing and managing my way around was easier than it had been at the community school. The racial and socioeconomic integration, coupled with a wise and inclusive culture that teachers and administrators modeled, created an environment in which students had a real chance to thrive.

It wasn't surprising that it didn't take long for my overall grades, including my conduct grades, to improve. Sure, there were still fights, but they were fewer and less intense. Everyone was better adjusted. Resources will do that.

For junior high, I returned to the neighborhood school, which more closely reflected the largely Black community in which I grew up. Importantly, the school bused in white kids. This brought resources and support from white families across the city. The culture was different, and that was good, too. While Vaughn Road had a white-dominated culture that Black kids learned to navigate, junior high had more Black culture that white kids learned to navigate. It was powerful to see your Blackness affirmed by most of your classmates and a lot of your teachers. In both cases, we enjoyed an excellent education.

That's not to suggest that it was all easy. Junior high is still adolescence.

I struggled to get comfortable in my own skin. In junior high, I wasn't as popular as I had been in elementary school. What makes you popular? Well, your athletic ability, for starters. I was still waiting for my growth spurt while the kids around me, boys, and girls, shot up in height and saw their body size increase. Of course, fashion and style meant a lot more in junior high than in elementary school. The popular kids had the newest clothes, rode motorcycles, and hung out with the older high school kids just above us. My parents didn't believe in spending money on the new and expensive fashion trends. And I sure as hell wasn't getting a motorcycle.

It was obvious from Jump Street that I wasn't going to sit at the top of the food chain in junior high.

I wasn't starting in football. I didn't make the basketball team. And I had stopped playing baseball. It was time to figure out a lot of stuff. In those years I started to lean in to student leadership activities, like student government, and got a lot more comfortable engaging and relating to others. It was there that my political awakening, which started in the Oldsmobile, began to intensify.

I first noticed the change in myself when I started paying more attention to my dad as I followed him to community centers and church basements throughout the state. Instead of tuning him out or goofing off with my brother, I started to listen to what he said in those rooms.

It slowly dawned on me that my dad was a disciple of Dr. King. He had known the man and worked under his leadership. He studied how he led and brought Dr. King's lessons into his leadership.

Dr. King always understood his audience. Understanding your audience begins with understanding what's important to them: their culture, their values, their beliefs. By knowing *who* he was speaking to, he was effective when speaking to groups of all sizes— from a national audience of millions, like the March on Washington in 1963, to much smaller groups that he encountered most nights during his travels across the South.

When addressing his audience, Dr. King made sure to understand *their context*. When he was in the South and immersed in Southern culture, he took care to understand the context of the Black *and* white audience members. This ensured that Dr. King didn't just "preach to the choir." It would have been easy, or at least convenient, to limit his speaking to Black audiences enthusiastic about the civil rights movement. But that wouldn't have made the biggest difference for the movement. Remember, in his lifetime Dr. King was unpopular. In any audience, there was a very good chance that many in attendance didn't fully agree or even like his message. Dr. King didn't shirk the responsibility; he leaned into it.

As a result, Dr. King was effective at disarming his opponents—in his case, the Southern white man, who was most often his critic and his enemy. To do so, Dr. King would strategically appropriate the segregationists' language of states' rights and fidelity to the Constitution above all else to write the destiny of Black Americans into the country's founding documents: the Constitution and the Declaration of Independence.

For example, according to the Constitution, we are entitled to our rights. And, like all people, we have the right to life, liberty, and the pursuit of happiness. By weaving the Black struggle into the founding language of the country, Dr. King was able to persuade a greater share of his audience than he would have otherwise.

Dr. King also famously leveraged the Bible and scripture. He was, first and foremost, a preacher, having grown up in the Baptist Church. To fight Mr. Segregation and Mr. Discrimination, he marshaled a legal case *and* a moral one. *That* was his essential strength. He articulated issues in ways that people could understand and in moral, and patriotic, language that moved them before mobilizing them to act urgently.

He was powerful.

Many political leaders choose between telling the truth or winning the day by telling people what they want to hear. Dr. King did *both*. He rejected the false choice between being right and winning. He did so by understanding his audience and his context before connecting the struggle of his people to language and terms that most resonated with his listeners' lived experiences and value systems. Ultimately, Dr. King wanted every American to embrace the notion that we're all American, entitled to the same rights and responsibilities.

I watched my dad use Dr. King's very same tools to rouse the city of Montgomery in the years after the civil rights movement. While Montgomery played a starring role in desegregating America, the city itself struggled to implement the changes it had initiated for the nation. The local backlash after the heyday of the civil rights movement was immense. When the city charter changed to pave the way for the election of Black officials, my dad ran and won. Because of those changes, he was among the first cohort of Black elected officials in Alabama since Reconstruction. But progress quickly gave way to pain, and Montgomery zagged after that.

Fearing the ascent of a Black political leadership, the backlash of the so-called New Right intensified. My dad struggled to mobilize voters and community leaders to remain hopeful and stay vigilant. Decades of activism had yielded the civil rights movement, and now, years after the Montgomery bus boycott, folks were fighting to prevent those wins from being snatched away. People were exhausted. They just wanted life to be okay, to no longer feel like a constant battle.

It all came to a head one night during a community town hall at one of the local high schools. My dad took Joey and me with him in the Oldsmobile. It was summer—hot—and the warm breeze funneled into the back seat. Joey and I argued whether the new Atlanta Brave, Dale Murphy, could pull the Braves out of the slump they had been in since the retirement of the great Hank Aaron. (I sided with 44 and argued that Dale Murphy couldn't hit a curveball.)

As we eased down the road, my dad was lost in his thoughts. The news played quietly on the radio. He slowly pulled into the parking lot. It was only half-full as we saddled up near the gym. Joey and I jumped out of the back seat and bounded up and down the parking lot in an impromptu game of tag. We were trying to squeeze in a little more fun before our dad started his remarks because we were old enough now to be expected to sit down and try to pay attention. As Dad ambled slowly into the building, I could sense his heaviness. He was usually excited to go into the community, but tonight it was clear that he dreaded having to give this speech. Looking back, I think it's because he knew he needed to deliver hard truths. This was the part of leadership that was about bearing the cross, not just wearing the crown.

After a short meet and greet, my dad saying hello to familiar faces, he made his way up to the makeshift stage and started his remarks.

"There were five days between Palm Sunday and the crucifixion," he started slowly. "Five days." He paused. "And on Palm Sunday, a crowd gathered outside and uttered, 'Hosanna, hosanna,' as Jesus entered Jerusalem. They put down the palms, they put down their coats, they put down just about everything they had to make the way for Jesus.

"All of this happened on Palm Sunday," he intoned.

"Then, that Friday"—his reedy voice was rising—"that same crowd was yelling, 'Crucifixion.' And when they had a chance to free Jesus or Barabbas, the thief, they chose to free Barabbas."

Suddenly he stopped. As if fully awake for the first time.

"We must be very, very careful. The Bible tells you, 'What does it profit a man to gain the world and lose his soul?' I ask you tonight: What does it profit to gain the nation and lose your city?"

That speech marked an important moment for me. *Lose your city?* What did he mean?

After the 1960s, Montgomery changed the country forever and for good, but Montgomery in the 1980s was at risk of sliding backward. The backlash from the New Right was real, and they were succeeding in putting Mr. Discrimination back in charge of writing, passing, and implementing our laws. Worse yet, our people were tired. Many had marched and protested and suffered for the better part of a decade. They might have started in the movement as bright-eyed college-age kids, but they were now fully formed adults with families to care for and bills to pay. Social activism pays where it counts most—it uplifts the inherent dignity of all people—but it doesn't keep the lights on.

Nevertheless, my dad was emphatic in his message to that tired audience: if we didn't stay vigilant, then we risked losing all the ground for which we had fought and sacrificed. We needed to find a second wind, and fast.

"It's time for a lot of the youngsters to step up as well," my dad continued. "Many of our children are at the age when they should share in these concerns. If your feet are tired, I get it. But we've got young, tender feet that should be taking to the streets."

For the first time in my young life, my dad, wearing the cape of Prominent Political Leader, was speaking to *me*. Shortly thereafter, Hank Aaron, the slugging superhero of the Atlanta Braves, number 44, came to visit my dad at the family home.

I was beyond hyped at the chance to meet one of my heroes, Hammerin' Hank himself.

"Steven, this is Hank Aaron from Mobile," my dad said as he introduced us. I looked up at Mr. Aaron and shook his big hand. I stared wide-eyed at the giant of a man standing before me. My dad's words turned over in my young mind.

Hank Aaron from Mobile.

Hank Aaron from Mobile.

Hank Aaron from Mobile.

Then it hit me. Hank Aaron identified as an Alabamian. Not as an Atlanta Brave or even a baseball player but an Alabamian. And he was here tonight, in our home, to support the movement: he cared that we didn't lose the progress we had fought so hard to achieve for Black people here in Alabama and across the South. I didn't realize it then, but later, as an adult, I would learn about the racism—the threats and the taunts and the bullying—that Mr. Aaron endured as the highest-profile Black American in a sport that had resisted integration. Mr. Aaron was, above all else, a leader. And like any great leader, he had sacrificed for the cause.

If *Hank Aaron* cared—about Mobile, about Montgomery, about Alabama, *about us*, all of it—then I needed to pay more attention to what was happening in our community and in our streets. Sports wasn't all there was to life.

I started to hear the call. My all-consuming passion for sports began to balance with an active interest in the community around me. I started to look at the people and places surrounding me with new eyes. It was uncomfortable, at least at first.

I grew more interested in my peers—where they were from, what their lives were like. I started to discover that I had some political talent. When I set my mind to it, I was a good listener, because I was interested. And it turned out I was interested in pretty much everyone and everything. I was forever curious.

I learned that I could relate and get along with middle-class Black kids and middle-class white kids. I learned that I could have friends, Black and white, who were upper class. I always had friends who grew up less fortunate, some living in public housing, and I strengthened those bonds. I also grew more aware that life was harder for them—they were overcoming hurdles and barriers that I didn't necessarily encounter in my own life. I grew more conscious.

In algebra, I sat next to a bank president's daughter. She was also white. In history class, I sat next to a housekeeper's son. He was Black. In school, we weren't segregated by race or class. We weren't separated. We had enough white students in our school to ensure that there were resources from wealthier white families pouring in, which benefited kids of all races.

We learned to talk to everyone as our school's diversity shaped every single student's experience. We listened to heavy metal. We dug rock and roll. When rap came onto the scene, we got into that. While we didn't fully appreciate it then, from class to class, moment to moment, we were engaged in nonstop cultural exchange, and all of us were better as a result.

To this day, I'm comfortable in any setting. It doesn't matter where anyone went to school because I've been fortunate to build relationships and to learn from people from every conceivable walk of life since an early age. That's why integrated, well-resourced public schools are so important. They facilitate the kind of society that we strive for but too rarely observe today—a world in which people are truly assessed based on the content of their character rather than on race or socioeconomic status.

It's funny: during this time, when I talked to my cousins in Chicago, Detroit, or parts of New York and New Jersey, they were surprised that my siblings and I attended integrated schools. They were surprised because their schools were not integrated in Chicago. Later, when I made it to Morehouse, most of my classmates had either gone to all-Black schools or they were the only Black students in some suburban or private school. It didn't matter if they grew up in California, Texas, or Ohio.

✳ ✳ ✳

My father always had a saying: "Watch what people do rather than listen to what they say." A lot of people say they value education. A lot of folks swear that children are our future. People say a lot of things. But it's our actions that count.

Montgomery's schools today are very different from the schools I attended when I was growing up. Far from the integrated schools I experienced, today's public schools are largely segregated by race, and many of the white families have pulled their children out of the public schools altogether, taking their resources with them.

A lot of the private schools are effectively segregated academies that are overwhelmingly white.

How did we get here?

In 1954, when the Supreme Court handed down its decision in *Brown v. Board of Education*, just 6 percent of Black students attended integrated schools. In the decades that followed, I and so many others benefited from the promise of integrated schools. People like my dad fought like hell to create that opportunity.

In the early 1960s, the Alabama State Teachers Association, the institution my dad led as executive secretary, fought to protect Black teachers and students from the nonstop machinations of white segregationists who were avowed defenders of the status quo. They viewed integration as the "Black invasion" and would stop at nothing to keep Black kids just like me from rubbing shoulders with their sons and daughters. They truly believed that they were "saving" the schools.

On the one hand, there wasn't a state in the union that didn't experience backlash in the years after segregation ended. But when Mr. Segregation died, his son, Mr. Discrimination, took his place. Segregationists used every tactic available to stem the tide of progress. In no place was that opposition more powerful than in Alabama, where it took no fewer than five court orders over the span of a decade to desegregate the schools.

Beginning in those years, white families would vote with their feet. After Tuskegee's public high school became integrated, every single white student withdrew from the school, leaving behind just twenty Black students. Governor Wallace closed the school shortly thereafter due to "economic liability." Between 1970 and 1971, more than 20,000 white students fled the public schools in the state of Alabama. Many of those families sent their children to private schools, taking their financial resources with them.

Since my days as a public school student, the number of resources flowing into Montgomery's public schools has continued to decline. In 1994, the city voted on a referendum that would increase funding for city schools—for the first time in decades—as a countervailing measure to the schools' broader demographic and related funding changes. The measure failed.

Meanwhile, Greater Montgomery grew stronger, often at the expense of the city. Communities like Prattville and Auburn, once tiny outposts, grew in stature as more middle-class families, especially military families, relocated there. Recently, I connected with a Black woman after a political event. She also serves in leadership at Maxwell Air Force Base and lives in Prattville. She expressed that she wanted to get involved in strengthening Montgomery, her hometown. I simply told her, "I need you in my city."

She stammered in response. She had left Montgomery because the schools are better in Prattville. It made more sense for her kids to live outside the city.

When she asked again how she could get involved in helping to turn around Montgomery, I simply reiterated, "I need you in my city."

The civil rights generation was never silent on issues of racial injustice, and throughout my life I saw civil rights greats like my father wear the crown of leadership and bear the cross to fight inequality up close. They fought for the big things. And they fought for the things that might not seem like a big deal through the prism of history but at the time made a huge difference for so many people.

Integrating the Y was one of those causes. Given the outsized role sports have played in my life, it's a cause that's close to my heart. And once again Montgomery played a starring role in an issue that reverberated nationally and changed the arc of history in America.

I grew up at the Cleveland Avenue YMCA in Montgomery, the very same Y where Dr. King was a member. The Cleveland Y was well known around town. During the '1950s, '60s, and well into the '70s, the Cleveland Y was referred to, often pejoratively, as the Black Y or the Y for Negroes. Dr. King himself, even as he was leading a nonviolent mass movement for racial equality, was forbidden from going to the Downtown Y (or the Central Y, as it's called today) because of his race. Across the South, from Montgomery to Atlanta and beyond, the Y stayed segregated.

While segregationists lost the battle to keep lunch counters, movie theaters, and public restrooms segregated in the 1960s, the fight to desegregate Montgomery's recreational facilities was stubbornly stuck. Desegregating recreational facilities, much like desegregating the schools, was viewed as a major threat to avowed white supremacists because it required integrating young people. An integrated recreational facility would expose young people to the common humanity that we all share. Through sports and competition, people would learn mutual respect.

It's hard to hate anyone up close, and it's hard to hate someone when you're guarding them in basketball.

To say the least, the segregationists got really, really worked up about integrating swimming pools, basketball and tennis courts, parks, and the like. And rather than abiding by court orders and federal injunctions, the city of Montgomery simply paved over all the public recreational facilities with dirt and closed them.

Just like that. Closed them all up.

The segregationists figured that they could opt into private facilities, just as white families had fled public schools to attend private academies in which they could exclude and evade Black people without inviting legal action. In short, the segregationists figured that they, along with their children, could re-create somewhere far away from any person with Black or brown skin.

But they miscalculated. Participation in the Y skyrocketed after the city closed all the public recreational facilities. It turned out that not every white person had the means or, frankly, the desire to attend a private, ultra-segregated facility.

So the fight for integrating the Y wasn't trivial. It wasn't small. There weren't many facilities where a Black child could learn or practice a sport or activity. For a lot of kids who grew up in my neighborhood, especially those of limited means, the Y represented a chance at escape—a path to a happier life and potentially a brighter future.

Fortunately, members of the community, white and Black, and leaders in business and the neighborhoods took the case all the way to the Supreme Court to prove that the Y indeed had a "municipal character." Although the Y was considered a private institution, it was, at its core, meant for the public, intending to serve all the kids. Therefore, any strictly enforced segregation violated the Civil Rights Act of 1964. This case represented one of the first instances in which a private organization—the realm in which most of our life occurs—was held to the same standards as public institutions such as schools and courthouses. Watching our community come together to do the right thing—and especially observing white community members using their voices to help others who were of a different race—was instructive for me as a Black kid growing up in Montgomery. It showed me that we could move past the racism that had poisoned our communities since forever.

My dad always did a good job of separating white supremacy from white people and was emphatic that we needed white people to end racism. He reasoned that if Black people could end racism on their own, we would have done it by now. Although my dad was what Julian Bond would term a "race man"—a Black man wholly dedicated to the struggle for Black liberation—my dad also partnered with and deeply trusted white people who were similarly dedicated. Indeed, the "merger," the legendary joining of the Black and white teachers associations in Alabama in the late 1960s,

followed five hard years of back-and-forth and only happened because of the bone-deep trust between my dad, a Black man, and
Paul Hubbert, a white man.

That merger was only possible because my dad took a radical
view of allyship. To paraphrase Dr. King, if your coalition is comfortable, it's too small. Throughout his career, my dad worked
hand in glove with others—even those with whom he didn't see to
eye to eye on every issue. His modus operandi was to align on
shared interests in a fight, expand his coalition as broadly as possible, and then *go win*.

That kind of allyship led to wins like the desegregation of the
Y. And my experience there was never distant from the civil rights
movement or the coalition of Black and white people who came
together to integrate one of the most important spaces in my
young life. I worked out there, played pickup games, forged close
friendships, and even got into more than a few fights. And because
it was desegregated, I learned to socialize and build relationships
across racial lines. Those were formative years.

By the time I started high school, I had emerged as a pretty good
athlete, in large part because of the Y. I started to turn my eyes toward college and think through what it might mean to play sports
at the next level. My social consciousness was evolving, too. As
much as I appreciated my father's call to my generation, the older I
got, the smaller Montgomery felt. I was questioning whether I was
cut out for a lifetime of civil rights activism in Montgomery or if I
should pursue a career, a calling, *whatever*, beyond the city.

By the time I finished my junior year of high school, I wanted
out of Montgomery. And not just for a spell but for good.

✳ ✳ ✳

I don't know the precise moment when my feeling toward Montgomery shifted, but the change started in high school. Part of it

was a natural extension of adolescence: What teenager doesn't rebel against the expectations under which they were raised? But part of it was the fact that my generation had a different perspective from that of our parents. A different perspective on both how to achieve change and what change meant.

It's easy to trace where that divergence started: the culture. When my parents came of age, television was in black and white—literally and figuratively. In those years, television portrayed a single, simplified perspective of the world. Moreover, television was largely a luxury item restricted to more affluent (mostly white) households. Most Black folks, on the other hand, consumed culture, got the news, and followed sports via the radio, which was either at home or usually in the local bar or restaurant. Very few Black families had access to television.

When people like my parents *did* watch TV, they encountered a world that was wholly whitewashed and broadcast on only four networks: CBS, NBC, ABC, and DuMont, which was gone in 1956. *Father Knows Best*, *Leave It to Beaver*, and *The Adventures of Ozzie and Harriet* set the pace as Hollywood followed the political climate of the day, which portrayed "normal" Americans as white, middle class, and embodying the values necessary to win the fight against communism: loving freedom, trusting elected officials, and, in general, not deviating from the norm.

Across the South, programmers at television stations worried that the very presence of Black people on their sets would turn off white audiences and foment a backlash in their viewership. Outside the South, it was only marginally better. The result: Black people rarely appeared on the television set. The deeper result? Television exacerbated the nation's racial divide. White people didn't view Black people as part of America's cultural fabric—which was painfully ironic, given the enormous cultural contributions of Black people. It's hard to overstate the extent to which

white people viewed Black people as culturally, socially, and economically *other*: Mr. Segregation was about more than the laws
and rules on the books. Mr. Segregation's grip on American life
was total and complete. It dominated the American experience.

The civil rights generation, of course, set out to change all that.
And television was one of their most formidable tools. Dr. King,
Rosa Parks, John Lewis, and the countless number of young activists who took to the streets to risk their bodies and lives understood, first and foremost, the power of images. The civil rights
movement scaled beyond a small group of devoted activists in
large part because Americans of all races were forced to bear witness to the horror of segregation: images of dogs biting, fire hoses
targeting, and billy clubs assaulting unassuming movement volunteers who were mostly students and retirees. Video of a tiny
Black school girl, Ruby Bridges, no more than five years old, walking bravely to school flanked by armed police, beamed into living
rooms across America.

In the end, *those* images propelled the movement.

The lack of representation in the culture helped to radicalize
my parents' generation against the total grip of Mr. Segregation.
How could it not? However, when I came of age in the 1970s, the
world was already very different. For starters, *everyone* had a TV.
And, thanks to pioneering producers like Norman Lear, there were
Black television shows like *Good Times*, *Sanford and Son*, and *The
Jeffersons* as well as *Star Trek* that were not only integrated but
showed Black people participating in a future that was awe-inspiring,
cutting-edge, and inclusive. For a period, Michael Jackson, on the
twenty-fifth anniversary of Motown, was all any teenager, Black or
white, wanted to watch.

In the 1970s, sports were also more integrated as Black representation mattered more and more, on and off the field. By the
time I was old enough to watch college football, for instance, Bear

Bryant had famously integrated the Alabama Crimson Tide and would go on to dominate college football for decades, a trend that continues to the present day.

The net result for my generation was an internalized sense of broader horizons. And by the time I was in high school, the world was big and inviting, and Montgomery was not.

It felt small. Antiquated. In its own way, stuck in the past.

My brother, Joey, broke out first.

When I was in the seventh grade, Joey, who was in high school, started thinking about college: tours, pamphlets, magazines, the whole bit.

At some point Joey decided he wanted to go to the University of Alabama. It's where his best friend from right up the street, John "Johnny" Winston, went. John came from a good, well-respected family. His dad was one of the first Black doctors in Montgomery and the only Black member of the school board. Another neighbor of ours also went to Tuscaloosa.

Their parents went to Alabama State, like ours. We were all living on the same street, which was just two blocks from Alabama State, but our friends wanted out, and many of them weren't called to attend an HBCU. At the time, part of the thinking was this: *Hey, our parents have done all this work to integrate the nation's finest colleges and universities, so shouldn't their children have the opportunity to attend the flagship schools?* It was a completely fair position that was common among Black families pushing their children to pursue a college degree.

So Joey came home one night for dinner and dropped the news on everyone.

"I want to go to Alabama," he said earnestly.

This time it was my father who was quick to respond.

"Nope." His tone was flat, matter-of-fact.

After he finished chewing his bite, he leaned back from his

plate and folded his napkin. "You're not going to the University of Alabama," his tone this time more insistent.

Joey started to protest, but my dad cut him off before he could start; his logic was clear and compelling if frustrating to receive.

"You don't need to go there, and they are not going to treat you right. You're carrying my name, and you'll have a target on your back from day one. It's out. No Alabama." The discussion was over, and Joey didn't have much to say for the rest of the meal.

I felt bad for him but understood where my dad was coming from. My dad was well connected and understood from his peers in the movement that their children hadn't had good experiences at Alabama. The old boys still controlled the state's flagship university, the sting of desegregation was too fresh, and the hostile work of Mr. Discrimination was in full swing.

After Joey had a few days to tend to his crushed dream, the subject of where Joey would go to school continued to bubble up over dinner.

"Why don't you think of Mo'house?" (My dad never said "Morehouse"; it was always "Mo'house.") Neither Joey nor I had considered or thought much about Morehouse. As lifelong Alabamians, we had been drilled in the histories of Montgomery and Birmingham, Alabama's major cities. Atlanta, really a sister city to Birmingham, sometimes felt like a world away. Sensing the disconnect, my dad set out to educate us about Morehouse.

"Well, look," he started, "Martin King went to Mo'house." (Dad had known Dr. King and had worked closely with him, but he never called him "Martin Luther King" or "Dr. King"; it was always "Martin King.") "Yep. Martin King went to Mo'house and his daddy went to Mo'house. Maynard Jackson went to Mo'house. Julian Bond went to Mo'house."

He paused.

"If Mo'house is good enough for Martin King, it's good enough for you."

Joey was silent; he was processing. Finally he responded, "Okay, we will go on some trips. We'll go visit some schools. Let's check out Morehouse."

Joey and my dad decided to visit several HBCUs across the South. I would tag along because it wouldn't be long before I needed to make my own decision about where to go to college. So, over spring break, we visited Florida A&M, Hampton, Morehouse, and Howard. By the time we left for the trip, Joey was excited about all of them. His infatuation with Alabama had worn off and the appeal of attending a school that was a national destination for Black excellence appealed to him.

We started off in Tallahassee before heading north. Once we hit Atlanta, we met one of my dad's friends from his organizing days, Lawrence Alfred, who greeted us on the Morehouse campus. I have since listened to several Morehouse alumni and administrators speak about the college since Joey first visited in 1987, but to this day, Lawrence Alfred probably made the most impactful remarks about Morehouse that I've ever heard.

Lawrence started simply, "Morehouse is a unique place for Black men. In fact, there's no other place in this world quite like it."

He continued in a low but urgent growl, "You'll never have another time where all the focus will be undeniably, unquestionably on you as a Black man to make you better and to make you successful in this white man's world."

That last sentence caught Joey by surprise. Joey was coming from Jefferson Davis High School, which, despite its name, was an integrated school, a place where interracial friendships were normal. Joey was arguably as comfortable with his white friends as he was with his Black friends. Up until that moment, neither of us had really thought about college like *that*.

Lawrence Alfred kept going: "Joey, let me tell you this in front of your brother and in front of your dad. If you don't want to be great, don't come here. *I don't want you to come here.* If you just want to get by and you just want to talk your way through stuff and do this and that, and be mediocre, then go somewhere else. Don't come here."

Joey and I were both speechless after that. The rest of the tour and the rest of the trip were a whirlwind, but the decision had been made. It was Morehouse or bust for Joey and, I knew then, for me, too.

Through it all, my dad never said a word. He knew.

Chapter 4

MORE THAN RACE

*W*e have Black politicians but we don't have Black wealth," I blurted out one morning over breakfast. I was a senior in high school now, almost an adult. With my older brother and sister out of the house, I enjoyed having more of my parents' undivided time and attention because I was developing my thoughts and ideas, trying on different identities—testing ideas about who I was and what I believed. I was reading a lot during this period and had grown more serious as a student. I enjoyed sparring more with my dad. He wasn't as intimidating to me as he had been when I was a child. And I was increasingly convinced that he wasn't right about *everything*.

I sopped up a plate of syrup with one of my mom's legendary buttered biscuits. This morning I was being intentionally provocative: I let the words hang out there as I watched for my dad's reaction.

"Sure we do," he countered, his tone a bit defensive. In response, he rattled off a few local Black business owners who ran restaurants, operated grocery stores, and drove taxicabs in and for our community. He went on to name several barbershops and funeral homes also owned by the Black community before I cut him off.

"Sure, we might have Black *businesses* but we certainly don't have Black *wealth*," I interjected. "How many Fortune 500 companies are headquartered in Montgomery? How many do we even control? Who makes the decisions here around real estate? The white people own the riverfront, while we're out here in the neighborhoods, struggling, barely making ends meet."

I was on a roll now. Words tumbled quickly out of my mouth in between big bites of buttered, syrup-drenched biscuits. "And it's bigger than that. When you go downtown and scan for the big buildings—the ones for the lawyers, accountants, and investment banks—they're not here, white or Black. Sure, we take out each other's laundry, we serve each other food, but at the end of the day we don't control the means of production or the money supply. We can't even play our hand, because we're not at the table."

The means of production. The money supply. A self-satisfied smile crossed my face. Those terms came from reading *Black Enterprise*, which I inhaled every month. All the studying was starting to pay off. I was growing more sophisticated in my arguments, and I knew it.

My dad's eyebrows cocked in displeasure but he stayed silent. My mom shuffled around in the kitchen, eavesdropping but taking care not to intervene. My dad silently finished his plate of scrambled eggs and Conecuh sausage. No buttered biscuits and syrup for him. I felt victorious. I had won the debate. It felt good to best my old man.

My interest in business and Black wealth had started innocently enough. Growing up around my dad, I steadily became more passionate about the civil rights movement. It was hard not to. It was what I was exposed to and it was impossible not to be inspired by the work of the movement. Like every young Black person growing up in Montgomery, I studied the civil rights heroes of my dad's generation: people like Fred Gray, Ralph Abernathy, and Rosa Parks, who had lived in Montgomery and made their mark on the city, and the nation.

Naturally, I gravitated toward Dr. King because he was the leader, and I read the parts of the history where most people start and unfortunately end their study of the movement: "I have a dream . . ." But in high school, as I went deeper into my studies, I learned about Dr. King's writings and speeches that he'd made toward the end of his life. I was struck by his opposition to the Vietnam War and by the Poor People's Campaign, which he waged until the day he was murdered in Memphis in April of 1968. I became obsessed with Dr. King's evolution. At the end of his life—at the tender age of thirty-nine—Dr. King was focused on questions that dealt with more than race. He focused on the yawning economic inequality that contributed to the oppression of poor people—of all races—everywhere.

When Dr. King traveled to Memphis, where he was struck down by an assassin's bullet, he did so to march in solidarity with local sanitation workers. Months earlier, two Memphis garbage truck collectors, Echol Cole and Robert Walker, were crushed to death by a malfunctioning truck. Their deaths were the latest in a string of accidents and tragedies that flowed from a systemic neglect of working people. In some ways, Dr. King's Poor People's Campaign represented the civil rights movement coming full circle as it returned to its roots as a labor movement focused on improving the economics of working communities—a movement that began with the sleeping car porters in the 1930s, '40s, and '50s.

This iteration of the movement, however, was characterized by Dr. King's emphasis on multiracial organizing. Better economics concerned everybody, including working-class white people. In Memphis, Dr. King mobilized not only Black workers *but also* poor white, immigrant, and American Indian communities to advocate for better economic conditions for themselves and their families. I loved that he cared about work and the dignity that comes from making money. We didn't just need civil rights; we needed economic justice, beginning with jobs and job creators.

I was *frustrated* that my dad didn't see that. Or if he did, he never talked about it. From my perspective then, he was still harping on the vote and the importance of electing Black politicians. But electing Black politicians wasn't the be-all and end-all. To change the destiny of the Black community—our respective family trees, for our children and our children's children—we needed resources. To put it bluntly: in America, Black people were wealth, but we hadn't figured out how to create it—not on any meaningful scale.

There were exceptions, of course. And they're important to name: A. G. Gaston in Birmingham. Herman J. Russell in Atlanta.

Chicago's John H. Johnson. Baltimore's William Lloyd "Little Willie" Adams. And entire communities of wealthy Black Americans, such as Prince George's County, Maryland, then (and still) one of the wealthiest zip codes of Black Americans anywhere in the country. Because of their contributions, those cities and communities— Birmingham, Atlanta, Chicago, Baltimore, and a large part of Maryland—emerged as epicenters of Black capitalism. It wasn't by accident, then, that more political control and cultural relevance followed. By the time I graduated high school, I was as inspired by leading Black capitalists as I was by the civil rights icons.

But those entrepreneurs, and those cities, were the exceptions. The rule was harsher and bleaker.

There was some convergence in the racial wealth gap immediately following the Civil War and the end of slavery. That made sense. Millions of Americans, previously enslaved, now owned their own human capital and thereby their means of production. Emancipation represented one of the largest "wealth transfers" in American history, if you want to think about it like that.

But by the mid-twentieth century, just as Black Americans started to capture dramatic political gains, our progress in closing the racial wealth gap came to a halt. That huge gap in the wealth of Black and white families has gotten slightly worse since the 1960s and has stayed stubbornly stable. In 2019 the typical white family had $184,000 in wealth versus $23,000 held by the typical Black family.[1] Overall, 82 percent of Black families held less wealth than the typical white family—a statistic virtually unchanged since the 1980s.

In practical terms, the racial wealth gap negatively impacts the length and quality of Black lives, which are shorter and less healthy on average. Our ability to ensure against setback or hardship is a fraction of what the typical white person is capable of. I saw it in my own community. Most of those small businesses my dad referenced— the restaurants, the grocers, the cabs—struggled to keep their doors open the second the economy faltered. When inflation gobbled up the purchasing power of the dollar in the early 1980s and when the recession of the early 1990s cratered consumer demand, it was *Black* businesses that shuttered first. When white America caught an economic cold, our community came down with financial pneumonia—and often the condition was terminal.

The racial wealth gap obviously impacted Montgomery, too. Everyone felt it. Landmark civil rights legislation and the election of Black officials for the first time since Reconstruction kicked off economically devastating white flight. Many white people were frightened by the political changes. Outvoted at the polling station, they instead voted with their feet—moving out of the city and igniting an explosion of wealthy suburbs across the state.

Montgomery struggled as its demographics transitioned. While other cities in the region capitalized on the opportunity flowing into the South starting in the 1980s and increasing throughout the 1990s, Montgomery struggled to keep up and adapt to the changing times. Multiculturalism was in—and attractive—and cities like Atlanta moved aggressively to market themselves as open for business, heralding a new era.

It wasn't for a lack of talent—Montgomery was and remains home to dynamic community leaders, entrepreneurs, and business owners—but our inability to move past the fights of the 1960s to come together and advance the city's shared interests was glaring. By the 1990s the toll of that disconnect was clear, and it was all the local opinion pages could focus on. Dilapidated buildings and abandoned homes marked Montgomery, while nearby communities blew up with suburban development and corporate relocations. The white tax base, now mostly moving out of the city, anchored the suburban communities surrounding the city, leaving the newly enfranchised Black community to grow its fragile financial stability on its own.

I was convinced that fixing the economics for Black Americans and Black cities was *the* answer—not just for Montgomery but for Black folks everywhere. My perspective was simple: we won the vote; *let's move on to secure our wealth and our futures.*

I viewed Morehouse as my chance to learn how to do just that. However, I didn't want to major in political science like my dad. And I definitely *did not* want to be a lawyer like my brother, Joey. And I was convinced that the law was a gateway drug to a career in politics, which I wanted to avoid at all costs.

So the plan was set. I would study finance and learn how to build wealth. I would use my summers to get a foot in the door of corporate America before taking a shot at entrepreneurship a few years out of school. From there, I would build a company that would set the world on fire, make me incredibly wealthy, and give me the platform to shape the fortunes of Black Americans everywhere. As for Montgomery, well, in my mind there wasn't any coming back to Montgomery. I would see my family and friends at Thanksgiving and Christmas. But outside of that, I was moving on to new places and to new people.

I was so excited to stand on my own two feet and to pursue my dream. But moving to Atlanta was about something deeper as well. At Morehouse, *I wasn't going to be someone's son.* It was my chance to start fresh.

Back in Montgomery, the winds of change were blowing, too. The fight for civil rights was ongoing. While Mr. Segregation was dead, Mr. Discrimination continued his reign of terror. White flight meant disinvestment from the local economy, but that didn't mean total abdication in local politics. The old boys still ran a lot of Montgomery and in many ways presided over the city's decline. They resisted investments in the public—our neighborhoods, our businesses, and our schools—because that would mean *investments in Black people.* The old boys wanted low taxes and minimal regulation so that the mostly white businesses that remained in Montgomery could carve out their little oasis with little to no interference while the broader community suffered.

The decline was most marked in the school system. Gone were the days when Joey and I enjoyed an imperfect but world-class public education in Montgomery. Our multiracial schools had been replaced by ones entirely attended by Black students who enjoyed just a fraction of the resources we did. The state of Alabama ratcheted up the "accountability," too—foreshadowing a larger educational reform movement in the decades ahead—as teachers worked tirelessly to educate a student body that was increasingly poor and in need of resources but with far less support.

It wasn't fair. My dad and his generation had fought so hard to bring about political equality. They succeeded but were met with a backlash. And now they had a bigger mess on their hands. For the schools, the only answer was more investment: teachers and principals were stretched thin, the facilities in which they taught were falling apart, and our students—many of them coming from distressed neighborhoods and unstable family environments—lacked the support necessary to reach their full potential. All this undermined confidence to invest in a system that very much *needed more investment*. Without more money, the schools would continue to fail to prepare their students for the world ahead.

My dad and other civil rights champions led the fight to increase the property tax investments in the schools. It was doomed from the start. For starters, any campaign *to raise taxes* must be messaged just right, and everyone playing a part in that campaign has to sing from the same sheet of music. The schools were struggling; that much was clear. But my dad's political coalition was at war with itself. They couldn't agree on anything, much less how to make a complicated but urgent case for investment. What was the winning message? My dad and his team never figured it out. In the end, the effort to raise taxes failed and the downward spiral of our schools continued.

The loss signaled my dad's political vulnerability, and a perfect storm for political change brewed. A few years later, my dad would lose his seat on the city council to Tracy Larkin. Like my dad, Tracy was a veteran who promised to bring change to the council. For my dad, it marked the end of a twenty-four-year career on the council, where he was last of the original city councilors elected in 1975. With his loss, one of Alabama's most powerful Black officials since Reconstruction no longer held his seat.

I was heartbroken for my dad. He'd worked his heart out for Montgomery and desperately wanted the city to have better schools so that our children could embrace a brighter future. But his grip on power was weakening and the headwinds he confronted too many. His loss reinforced what I had already concluded: Montgomery was stuck.

☀ ☀ ☀

Atlanta, on the other hand, was *moving*.

By the time I showed up for freshman orientation at Morehouse, Atlanta had transformed from a regional city into a national powerhouse.

And it wasn't inevitable. Atlanta in the 1950s through the 1970s struggled with the same dynamics that plagued most cities across the Deep South: the fight to end segregation; the turmoil over integration, including epic white flight; and a country that was deindustrializing and transitioning to the knowledge economy.

So, what was the difference between Atlanta and other cities in the Deep South? First, Atlanta moved decisively to integrate. It moved faster than a lot of Southern cities to embrace Black futures. But that's not to say there weren't challenges, setbacks, or what my dad would call "politricks."

Atlanta's trajectory toward a faster integration started right after World War II, when newly enfranchised Black veterans used their political sway to secure the presence of eight Black police officers on the force. Fifteen years before Bear Bryant integrated the Alabama Crimson Tide, the president of Georgia Tech resisted calls from Governor Marvin Griffin to segregate the Sugar Bowl when Bobby Grier integrated the game in 1956. The president's terse statement, "No Grier, no game," spoke volumes about the university's insistence to keep the politics of hate out of the game. Across Atlanta, there were enough people of all races in the public and private sector who embraced the city's informal motto, "The City Too Busy to Hate," that it led to earlier integration in the housing and job markets.

By 1973, Atlanta had its first Black mayor, Maynard Jackson, a Morehouse Man. Like most American cities, including Montgomery, Atlanta saw its fair share of challenges in the 1970s. However, the difference was that Mayor Jackson positioned Atlanta as a transportation and logistics hub, areas of the economy where the city already had a competitive advantage because of investments from the Second World War. As part of Atlanta's "modernization," Jackson invested in the airport and subway system, strengthening its capacity to bid on global opportunities like the Olympics, which it hosted in 1996, catapulting The A to international acclaim.

Atlanta's story proves that the South isn't monolithic. Cities across South Carolina, Georgia, Alabama, Mississippi, Arkansas, and Louisiana experienced the civil rights movement—and the decades that followed—differently. Ultimately, the cities that "won" in the years that followed integration managed to move past their divisive racial politics in order to seize a future that benefited everyone. Other cities, including Birmingham and Montgomery, remained mired in the past.

Through the 1970s and '80s, neither Montgomery nor Birmingham could get out of its own way: as our populations dwindled, our politics, divided and mired in racial polarization, couldn't propel city leaders to seize the opportunities of the future. Today it's a different story. My counterpart in Birmingham, Mayor Randall Woodfin, and I both draw inspiration from Mayor Jackson's example as we make an aggressive case to the world that our cities are worthy of investment. As an Alabamian, I am proud, for example, that Birmingham hosted the World Games in 2022, a massive achievement and a stepping-stone to bigger opportunities.

No doubt, Morehouse benefited from Atlanta's ascent. And the results speak for themselves. The titans of the civil rights movement and much of the city's political leadership were trained there. Morehouse created a culture of excellence and competence, which my dad hungered to see in Montgomery.

✳ ✳ ✳

When I arrived at Morehouse for freshman orientation, it was like being dipped in the Jordan River. Just like Naaman in the Bible, I felt *brand-new*, my slate wiped clean as I walked up the marble steps that mark the campus entrance. I was overwhelmed with a sense of possibility. And I was grateful for the *freedom* I suddenly felt: for the first time in my life, I wasn't Joe Reed's son. Morehouse was my chance to start over and build my identity from the ground up.

It was a different world. The first thing I noticed was that Black excellence was felt across every domain: the campus culture, the academics, the vibe, *everything*. That dynamic was refreshing. My high school was racially split, and although I enjoyed my time there, the curriculum was Eurocentric, with a big emphasis on the Greeks and the Romans and the impacts of Europeans on American life. Over time I found that tiresome, and it became increasingly clear that there was so much I wasn't being taught—about Black people and our history.

At Morehouse, I received a very different education. From the curriculum to the professors to the student body, my education affirmed pride in Black history and uplifted Black excellence. Simply being surrounded by thousands of Black men was affirming and a completely singular experience in my life up until that point. The young men of Morehouse came from cities that I had only read or heard rapped about: Los Angeles and Oakland, New York and Boston, Kansas City and St. Louis, Houston and Miami. Students flew in from around the world, too: Ghana, Nigeria, South Africa, and Barbados.

Day one at Morehouse was a little bit like showing up at an All-Star Game. After exchanging a few pleasantries, every single student would introduce himself with his biggest high school accomplishment: "I was valedictorian at my high school." "I was the captain of the basketball team." "I was student body president."

Everybody was somebody. And I *loved* it. I remember thinking, *All right, this is what's up.*

As an all-Black and all-male school, Morehouse created an immediate feeling of brotherhood. It was the first environment I experienced in which everybody addressed one another with "What's up, brother?" There wasn't the usual "What up, my nigga?" that I had come to expect from high school. This was different. Even the fraternities, especially the Ques, operated differently. I tried, for instance, to pledge Omega Psi Phi Fraternity, Inc. Although it didn't work out, I don't regret trying. The pledging process was engineered to make me a better man. It worked.

There was a level of conformity in that, too. I noticed right away that everybody had the same mindset along with a burning desire to leave their mark on the world. As we listened to orientation speakers, student leaders, administrators, faculty, and alumni, they all hammered home variations of the same theme: Whether it's medicine, academia, finance, the law—whatever it is—you're going back home to lead and to impact the Black community. You're here to prepare, and our job is to prepare you—prepare you to shape a world that wasn't necessarily built for you but now needs you. We expect you to go back to your cities and be leaders, not followers, not to perpetuate the status quo but to be agents of change.

The speakers also weighed the legacy of Morehouse in their remarks. And not just the go-to greats like Dr. King or Julian Bond. This was the training ground of Howard Thurman, Maynard Jackson, Walter Massey, David Satcher, Spike Lee, Samuel L. Jackson, and Edwin Moses, to name just a few. The legacy was exhilarating, but I also immediately felt the weight of responsibility. One speaker even closed his remarks with "This is what you're coming into. Don't mess it up."

I'll never forget the last night of orientation, when my roommates and I stayed up late processing what we had experienced that week. We were grappling with what it meant to be a "Morehouse man," turning over in our minds the fact that we now walked the same hallowed halls that many of our heroes had.

As we prepared to wind down for the night, there was a sudden knock on the door. An older student poked his head in and ordered, "Put on a white T-shirt and jeans and head outside. Now."

I was confused. It wasn't just raining, it was *pouring* outside. It was an *epic* thunderstorm. One that those of us who were there that evening still talk about. But we didn't question it. We got dressed and went out.

Before long, I was among six hundred guys running around the campus. I wasn't sure where we were going; I was just trying to keep up.

Finally, we went under a tent. Just soaked. All six hundred of us. We were awake now.

My brother, Joey, who had gone to Morehouse five years before me, warned me earlier that week, "Remember, Steven, you don't go to Morehouse; you pledge Morehouse." Sitting outside at 4:00 a.m. under a massive tent, soaking wet and shivering, among six hundred confused freshmen—I finally understood what he meant.

We were talking loudly, practically shouting, over the din of the thunderstorm. I barely made out what others around me were saying.

"Why are we here?" I yelled to the young brother sitting right in front of me. He simply pointed toward the front.

There, on a small stage, stood Jamal Harrison Bryant, today the senior pastor of New Birth Missionary Baptist Church, but then a senior at Morehouse with a booming voice.

"Shut up," he began. His tone forceful but measured.

I was near the front, and our lot immediately complied. But the guys in the back couldn't hear him. The murmuring continued. "Shut up!" he said again, this time louder. Those farther back began to simmer down before Jamal yelled again, this time with thundering force: "*Shut up!*" He ripped his T-shirt off.

He had our attention now.

We were silent. "Leaders are made here," he started, before launching into a sermon about the power and importance of Morehouse. His words, his presence, everything about him, was riveting and unforgettable. His words echoed a lot of what we had heard already, but it was the context and his presentation that made the lasting impression: Jamal, standing there shirtless, lightning striking behind him in the sky, thunder rumbling. We sat there cold and shivering, bleary-eyed but *inspired*. And ready. For anything. For everything. It was something right out of a movie.

Years later, when Jamal was delivering a sermon at Dexter Avenue King Memorial Baptist Church here in Montgomery, I walked up to him afterward and simply said, "Shut up."

He looked at me, confused. "What's that?" An awkward pause ensued before I finally let out a roar of laughter. "Spirit Night, 1992."

Jamal busted out laughing. "Man, y'all killing me."

He had made a big impact on me and my friends. We talk about it to this day.

"Man, listen," I said. "My boys Rob, Darius, Joe Rob, KJ—all of them are education, corporate, entrepreneurial, and faith leaders operating at the highest levels. All of them. Hell, I run the city of Montgomery. But when we get together now, all we can talk about is Spirit Night and Freshman Week."

Academic excellence was a huge part of Morehouse. During Freshman Week, speaker after speaker quoted Dr. Howard Thurman: "Over the heads of her students, Morehouse holds a crown that she challenges them to grow tall enough to wear."

Start to finish, Morehouse was a roller coaster. There were a lot of highs, lows, and bewilderment in between.

As my mom called out early, I had a habit of talking my way in and out of stuff, which was especially true at school. When I was younger, I would debate or argue with the teacher about a grade on a homework assignment or even a test. I knew how to be persuasive. Growing up around my dad taught me to be comfortable negotiating with authority. That changed when I got to Morehouse.

The teachers were unbreakable. With them, there was no talking in or out of anything. They were religious in their commitment to preparing us to perform at the highest level. Most of my professors at Morehouse said at one time or another, "We're preparing you for Yale, Harvard, Columbia. We're preparing you for the elite schools, to represent us, and we're going to get you trained and ready to represent us at the highest level mentally."

That dedication showed up everywhere. When I got my first college paper back, one of the comments in bright red ink said, "This is supposed to be a colon, not a semicolon." When I went to dispute the comment with Dr. Anne Watts—and the five points she deducted from my grade as a result—she didn't budge.

"It's a semicolon," I pleaded. "What's the difference? You're going to take off five points for that?"

"It's all the difference in the world" was the only thing she said. While it wasn't her first rodeo, it was mine. I learned then and there that a lot of what I was used to from my high school education wouldn't fly at 830 Westview Drive. Indeed, Morehouse was most like the education—the care, the professionalism—that my mother drilled into us at home. Up until that point I had always struggled to make those habits from my mom stick. Morehouse called that out in me, and suddenly her years of training and preparation clicked into place, because the environment and the culture wouldn't accept anything less.

The House challenged me, and I was better for it. I also observed that each of my peers worked from a different set of gifts and ambitions. Some students were naturally brilliant. They could play *Spades, Dominoes,* or *John Madden Football* all day, all night, and then bust a 95 or a 98 on a big test or exam. Others worked all the time and struggled to excel no matter how hard they tried. Some *thought* they could play *John Madden* or cards and ended up dropping out: their desire to fit in with the perceived cool kids overwhelmed any need they might have felt to apply themselves.

I was somewhere in the middle. I worked hard at school, and the environment brought out the best in me. Before Morehouse, I was a good student but not a great student. College showed me that I could perform with the best if I worked at it. For the first time in my life, I applied a valuable lesson I had long internalized from sports to my academics: Ignore the grades—the external scoreboard—and focus instead on your effort. Work smart and hard. Working hard for hours on end without a clear sense of what you are working toward means diminishing returns on your effort. But getting clear on where you need to prepare, focusing there, and working until you get it right—that makes a difference.

My newfound work ethic dovetailed with an education that opened my eyes to a richer, deeper tradition of Black excellence. Before Morehouse, African history was a black box. Even growing up with the parents I was blessed with, I didn't know the history of Africa. High school overwhelmingly hewed to a Eurocentric model of history and culture. The History of World Civilization, taught by Dr. Lester Rodney, was a fascinating class because he showed us all that Africans had achieved and contributed to human progress. Imagine my surprise when, after four years of learning Latin in high school, I learned that the Egyptians had pioneered trigonometry, calculus, and logic thousands of years ago.

It's funny: the very politicized conversation around critical race theory makes me chuckle because most of my education in the South was effectively whitewashed by omitting the thousands of years of contributions by Black people worldwide.

We weren't exposed to Black authors in literature, either, growing up in the South. Interestingly, friends of mine from big cities in the Midwest, in the Northeast, in the Mid-Atlantic states, and on the West Coast had consumed so much more Black literature by the time they arrived at college.

When I speak to school leaders in Montgomery today, I always emphasize that if they don't show Black children that there were people who looked like them and had been making literary contributions for centuries, and if all they're exposed to are white writers, it creates a disconnect. It's hard for any student to maintain a passion for reading and learning if they can't see themselves in the content. That's why representation is so important.

I experienced the impacts of representation at Morehouse. Seeing myself in my studies, really for the first time, motivated me to try harder at school and to learn more. I also realized that a lot of my ambivalence toward school early on stemmed from a lack of connection with the material and with many of my teachers.

Growing up in Montgomery, I obviously knew the history of the civil rights movement backward and forward, but the broader context of Black history was virtually nonexistent in my education before college. With that context, I gained a new appreciation for what my parents' generation accomplished in the American South when I realized that we were part of a global community with a long and rich history of both struggle and triumph. For a while I even seriously considered majoring in English or history. I ultimately settled on business because of my passion for extending the gains of the civil rights movement through economics, but that grounding in *our history* never left me.

As I settled into my studies, I was hell-bent on learning how to succeed as an entrepreneur.

One of my most memorable experiences came from my finance seminar with Professor John Williams. Professor Williams was legendary at Morehouse. He was, as we said then, one of the best professors to grace the campus. He literally wrote the textbook on finance taught at the business school. His teaching style was different: it modeled life in the corporate world. He taught according to the case method. Every class, he randomly called on student after student, and how you performed there was at least half of your grade. There was no fooling Dr. Williams. You either knew the material and were ready to engage or you didn't. There was nowhere to hide.

Socially, Morehouse was *School Daze*. Hip-hop increasingly defined the cultural mainstream and campus life: Tribe, 2Pac, and OutKast. A lot of rappers who would go on to conquer the worldwide charts dominated the Atlanta college scene in those years. Bounce music was everywhere. Luke, Kilo Ali, DJ Jimi, and the So So Def family. We'd watch those guys on *Rap City* on Black Entertainment Television in our dorms, and a few years later they were on MTV.

Fast-forward to when my daughter left to study at Howard, I shared with her that one of the most important things about attending an HBCU is the opportunity to live at the forefront of Black culture—a culture that has a major influence on American culture. Whether it's Hampton or Howard, Morehouse or Morgan, performers of all stripes come to the HBCUs first to see how their art plays with the young audience of influencers. If the latest R&B or hip-hop artists sell there, then there's a very good chance they'll dominate the charts nationally. That's one of many special things about going to a college that centers Black culture.

I knew from firsthand experience. All the hip-hop acts from across the country came through Atlanta and would perform at Morehouse, Clark Atlanta, Morris Brown, or Spelman. In the early '90s, you could literally see Biggie Smalls at the Warehouse on a school night. A lot of up-and-coming talent came through, too, and they would give away or sell their CDs cheap. Some of those rappers were out of the South, like 8Ball & MJG from Memphis, or Scarface and the Geto Boys out of Houston. I didn't know them at the time, but participating in that culture and having a front-row seat to watching hip-hop take shape and eventually dominate American culture was incredible.

My biggest revelation in college? My appreciation for the beauty of Black women.

Sure, I had noticed their beauty before, going to public school back home. Or at least I *thought* I knew what it was. Growing up, I all but lived on the campus of Alabama State University, home to extraordinarily beautiful Black women. You also could have gotten your hands on *Essence* magazine or tagged along to go to the Ebony Fashion Fair with your mom or sister. But in the Atlanta University Center (or AUC, as we called it), I truly understood, for the first time in my life, the full and complete diversity of Black female beauty, spanning all shades, dark and light, tall and short, petite, thick, and all gorgeous. And *smart*. Like, *real smart*. I learned early on that I couldn't be lazy with a young sister and expect to enjoy any success. The AUC was replete with beautiful women who were also incredibly serious scholars, intent on taking their seat at the table of future leaders.

At orientation during my first week at Morehouse, I remember when they opened the gates to Spelman, which adjoined our campus, and their freshman class spilled out onto the shared parking lot. We each got paired with our Spelman "sister." That whole experience was akin to Revelations. Eye-opening, to the say the least.

There was competition, too. Morehouse wasn't the only college in Atlanta with men, and all of us were vying for attention from these bad sisters. We got schooled, early and often, on how to proceed when older students would remark, "All right, if you go over to another campus, then you've got to go with some of your boys from the floor of your dorm. Whatever you do, don't go over there by yourself," because invariably a turf war would break out.

And it did. Often. Fights would break out. It almost always started like this: "Y'all couldn't get into Morehouse." And then it was *on*.

Or it went like this: "Y'all Morehouse dudes are whack." It was *on again*.

It always started that way, but it almost always finished like this: "Oh, we're from the same hometown," or "We're both from the same area in the South," and suddenly we made a friend for life.

✳ ✳ ✳

I played and lettered in football in high school and eventually college. At Morehouse, I played Division II football—not the D-1 but serious stuff. I learned a ton and worked as hard as I ever worked on the field. I played defensive back. Depending on who you ask, I wasn't good enough to be on the offensive side of the ball, so the coaches stuck me on defense. Also, depending on who you ask, I couldn't catch the ball very well. I can neither confirm nor deny that.

But what I *did* have as a player and why I went on to lead and letter on a collegiate football team at a high level of competition was *vision*. A good defensive back must *see* the field: What plays are unfolding? Where is the offense going with this play? The next play?

Playing defense taught me that, on and off the field, you can always overcome your shortcomings with the right level of effort and, more importantly, *attention*. When I counsel a young person, I encourage them to really pay attention to not just what's happening in front of them but all around them. Be observant. Try to pick up on the schemes that inform and organize our lives. Don't accept anything at face value. Understanding not only what's happening but where the opportunities and vulnerabilities are. Paying attention and truly understanding are more important than any one action.

The lesson doesn't stop there. A great defensive back also marries vision with *mindset*. Defense is always about shaking off the last play in order to put your best foot forward in the play that's coming. You have to be mentally tough and undeterred by setbacks. With very rare exceptions, the best defenses usually give up some points in the game. The difference is whether you bounce back from having fallen short.

For whatever reason, I was cut out to be a strong defensive back. I had vision and I had mindset.

My only challenge throughout my football career? I was small. That growth spurt that everyone talked about in the fourth, fifth, and sixth grade never really happened for me. Sure, I got a little bigger and stronger, but I am, to this day, just like my dad: a slight guy. But I made up my mind a long time ago that I wouldn't let size deter me. When I was in grade school—the first one, with my neighborhood buddies—I learned that if I let size get in my way, I would never, ever have any fun. I would always sit on the sidelines.

That meant getting used to pain. Getting hit, knocked down, pushed around—all of that comes with the territory when you're smaller than the other guys. But I learned something profound: *getting hit isn't that bad.*

Don't get me wrong: getting hit isn't fun. And I am certainly not glamorizing it. But it wasn't that bad. I survived. I got back up. And if I maintained my mental toughness, I lived to see another play during which my strengths—my vision and my mindset— could shine.

I discovered something else through all this: that resilience and mental toughness translated outside of the locker room, too. Football, for all its physicality, is a mental sport. And a football team is like any other team: its culture as well as the morale and performance of the organization are impacted by the behavior of each member of the team. Every player matters, and even a few unmotivated or toxic players can drag the whole team down.

My freshman year, our college football team was bad. We went just three and seven on the season. That means we won only 30 percent of our games.

The next season I came back ready to compete. My attitude was simple: We may not win every game, but let's fight and com- pete every time we take the field. And I wasn't even a starter at that point, which was okay because I learned a lot from watching other players who were older and better than me. Vision in leadership starts with vision in followership.

But others on the team didn't share my intensity. It was frus- trating. So finally I did what I had watched my father do all my life: I used my voice.

It was in the locker room after an especially dispiriting prac- tice. The season hadn't even started yet, but it felt like we were al- ready settling for less than our best. I couldn't stand it.

"Y'all, if we're going to turn this around, then we need to

compete harder. We're not working hard enough out there. This year is going to be just like last year."

I didn't know who I was speaking to, specifically, but it needed to be said. I was met with shrugs and grunts, but I saw recognition in some of the eyes of my teammates. Together, we started to shift the culture of our team by leaning in to our actions, what we could control. Belief in a bigger goal and a work ethic are contagious. Before long, our team started to recapture some mojo. We went six and five that season. We didn't light the conference on fire, but we proved to everyone and, most importantly, ourselves that we could compete.

Don't be afraid to stand tall. Understand that sometimes you're going to be on an island. Doing what's right isn't always popular. My dad has modeled that all through his career. Often, when we study extraordinary leaders, like Dr. King, we mythologize and sanitize their contributions. This is a mistake, because whether we realize it or not, portraying them as unidimensional statesmen who were widely loved and uncontroversial during their lifetimes is misleading.

Dr. King stood for more than the Dream. He stood for inconvenient, uncomfortable truths. Since his death, our society has achieved only a fraction of the change Dr. King called for during his lifetime. Even while he was alive, Dr. King minimized the achievements for which he is most famous today. A year before his death, in a speech called "The Other America," Dr. King recognized that "it's more difficult today because we are struggling now for genuine equality. And it's much easier to integrate a lunch counter than it is to guarantee a livable income and a good solid job."

Dr. King died struggling for economic justice for all people. He died leading demonstrations that were, at the time, deeply unpopular. Much like the calls against the demonstrations in Kenosha after the shooting of Jacob Blake, or Minneapolis after the killing of George Floyd, Dr. King confronted a media and an electorate that were more concerned with the destruction of property than with the loss of life. In his "Letter from Birmingham Jail," Dr. King pulled no punches when he addressed the country's majority that was unhappy with his activism and tired of the seemingly never-ending civil rights movement: "You deplore the demonstrations taking place in Birmingham. But your statement, I am sorry to say, fails to express a similar concern for the conditions that brought about the demonstration."

I am not encouraging violent demonstration. I am not calling for lawlessness. Indeed, Montgomery was one of the few cities that was entirely peaceful during the racial justice reckoning that swept the country after the tragic and brutal murders of Breonna Taylor and George Floyd.

But the core of my point stands. As my father said, many times, "You want to remember that the hottest place in hell is reserved for those who maintained their neutrality in a time of moral crisis." Growing up, I internalized the lesson. As a young person, I learned to live by it, first on the field, and eventually, off.

Ultimately, impactful leadership is not only hard, but it's often controversial and unpopular. You'll find that in your own life, at any level at which you lead, from the sports team to the classroom, in the workplace and in the boardroom. Great leaders often sacrifice popularity and social acceptance in advancing what's right.

This was a common theme in speeches and remarks by great civil rights leaders. In 1966, Bobby Kennedy gave a speech at the University of Cape Town. As he addressed the students there, many active in the struggle to topple apartheid, Kennedy highlighted the importance of youth in social change. He defined youth not as "a time of life but a state of mind, a temper of the will, a quality of imagination, a predominance of courage over timidity, of appetite for adventure over the love of ease." He reminded those in attendance that across history *it was young people* who often found the courage to stand up to convention to do what was right. Martin Luther was a young monk when he launched the Protestant Reformation; Joan of Arc was just nineteen when she extended the territories of France; Thomas Jefferson was just thirty-two when he penned the words *all men are created equal*.[2]

Indeed, Martin Luther King was just thirty-four when he bellowed, "I have a dream . . ."

The most telling passage in Kennedy's speech spoke to the importance of moral courage:

"Few are willing to brave the disapproval of their fellows, the censure of their colleagues, the wrath of their society. Moral courage is a rarer commodity than bravery in battle or great intelligence. Yet it is the one essential, vital quality for those who seek to change the world—which yields most painfully to change."[3]

I was lucky to observe a lot of moral courage growing up. As I came of age, I slowly learned to embody it in my own leadership.

But often courage begins with your own choices about your own life. And I struggled mightily with my desire to carve out my own path with a competing urge to fit in and follow the crowd. That only grew harder when it wasn't *obvious* what I would do while my peers participated in more conventional and well-defined paths. This came to a head during my junior year as most of my classmates opted into consulting and investment banking. The same contrarian streak that had me resisting the "family business" of law and politics coming out of high school compelled me to turn down opportunities that I felt were too traditional. I heard another calling. I believed that our communities needed to build Black wealth. And I knew that entrepreneurship was one way to accomplish that goal. But even after three years of Morehouse, I still wasn't exactly sure how to get the experience, networks, or access I needed to make that dream a reality.

In this area, Morehouse wasn't helping. Morehouse has so many positive attributes, but a negative one is that the environment is conservative with a small *c—it's traditional*. Most Morehouse men pursue the more conventional path, where they go on to have a lot of success after paying their dues and climbing the ladder. My peers were no different. As my friends accepted offers at Goldman Sachs, J.P. Morgan, and Arthur Andersen, I started to feel a tinge of regret. That only got worse when some of my friends announced that they were going on to graduate school. Had I made a mistake? By turning down the usual paths, I was beginning to wonder if I had jumped out of a plane without a damn parachute. What the hell was I going to do?

The truth is I couldn't have done anything else. It wasn't who I was. I was impatient. And in my heart I wanted to be an entrepreneur. I wanted to build big businesses and bring opportunity to communities where there wasn't any. While I wanted big-business experience to equip me for the entrepreneurial path, I wasn't sure where to turn for that experience. Silicon Valley then wasn't what it is today, and most operating companies had yet to build recruitment pipelines at HBCUs or in the Deep South. Consulting and banking had a huge presence on campus, but the work was too detached. It didn't take long to conclude that your fingernails never got dirty when you went to work there. Worse yet, the starting salary of $49,000 (!) brought along with it the proverbial "golden handcuffs." I knew too many guys around my brother's age who started in corporate America, planned to do it for a few short years, and nearly a decade later were still in it. I was always good at sensing a trap.

My internships were also a mixed bag. By turning down the usual options in Big Consulting and at the marketing companies, I didn't have much else to choose from. By the start of the summer after my junior year, my embarrassment and insecurity from not having a better plan got the best of me. I skipped the senior trip, which undoubtedly would have been a great time, and headed home to take a gig back in Montgomery.

The internship was at an investment shop specializing in municipal bonds. I knew the CEO of the firm and considered him a friend and a mentor. I figured I could build my competence and confidence in finance for a summer while charting my next move. The only downside was that the internship also put me back in Montgomery. I figured a summer at home wouldn't kill me, and besides, I wasn't exactly tripping over myself to hang with my buddies on vacation. I wasn't feeling settled, and maybe some time at home would do me good.

Not long after I started, Bill, the CEO, took me to lunch. We went to a local taco joint—one of those greasy spoons that makes damn good tacos you enjoy in the moment, only to regret them later. It was hot, and as we sat there sweating through our dress shirts and suit pants, Bill pressed me on my plans.

"So, what are you going to do?" he started. I explained that I wanted to build a career in corporate America before eventually moving into entrepreneurship. We needed Black wealth in our communities, I emphasized, and building big businesses in the Black community was the only way.

"Is Montgomery in your future? We sure could use that kind of energy and hustle here," Bill said. I was on my second taco at this point and my stomach was already grumbling.

"I ain't coming back here. I ain't never coming back here." I was a bit agitated at the suggestion. It honestly could have been the tacos. Whichever it was, in that moment I was emphatic.

And Bill was surprised. Unsatisfied. "What about politics? Your dad says you're a natural." I was surprised by the compliment. *A natural?* Dad never said that to me.

Bill pressed further. "We need leaders who understand where

we come from and know how to work with the business community to create opportunity. To your point, that is the next leg of the civil rights movement. You could be that leader."

I snorted. I was incredulous. "I sure as hell ain't coming back here to be no politician. You can forget about that." I felt a familiar sermon building deep in my spirit. Bill needed to hear the Talk.

I took a long drink of my Coke, took a deep breath, and then started. "You see, Bill, *I am the other PK.*"

"What's *the other PK?*" he asked, amused.

"Like the 'preacher's kid,' *the PK*. I am *the other PK: the politician's kid*. What you've got to understand is that I've been in every community center, every church basement, every chicken fry, bull and oyster roast, bingo night, carnival, and county fair in the whole damn state of Alabama."

Bill laughed. I got even more worked up. *He thinks I am joking,* I thought. I kept going, I was wound up now.

"To boot, I've been to more city council meetings, marches, protests, and demonstrations—before the age of thirty—than most people attend in their entire lives. And I paid—and I still pay—a price. When I walk into a bank or the grocery store, go get my hair cut, go to a restaurant—hell, even go to the bathroom—everyone knows who I am, who my dad is, and what our connection is to the burning issue of the day.

"*Steven, when are you and your dad going to do something about the schools?*"

"*Mr. Reed, we need more jobs in this part of town. When you see your dad, ask him about it.*"

"*Steve, the violence is just too much. Y'all have got to do something.*"

"Every problem," I continued, this time in a low whisper, "is *my problem*, and, worse yet, when I am here, people won't let me have an identity outside of my dad's. *It's exhausting.*"

I took a deep breath and sat back. Bill had stopped eating his tacos at this point. He looked at me earnestly, genuinely interested in what I had to say next.

"I agree with your premise," I continued, matter-of-factly. "This city is stuck. It needs new leadership and a new perspective. Instead of settling yesterday's issues, we've let the past define our future. Our history is a nightmare we never wake up from. And we lost sight of the whole point: life is for living, and our people can't live out here—not like this. Where are the jobs? The resources? Where's the hope?

"I am not sure there is any," I finished. "What did LBJ say? *'You can't make chicken salad out of chicken sh-t.'*"

I paused dramatically. "And these tacos sure as hell ain't changing the game, either." We laughed, easing the tension.

Bill heaped another helping of rice and beans on his clean "happy plate."

He carefully measured his words. "Steven, I hear you and I understand. I'm just telling you, I think you could be Montgomery's first Black mayor. I think you ought to think about it."

"Bill—" I started, an edge to my voice.

He cut me off with a wave of his hand as he took a long swig of Coke from a bottle. "I know, *'the other PK.'* Let's get back to the office."

A summer of investment banking in Montgomery, getting drilled on finance, yield curves, and fixed income derivatives, was enough for me. My plan for the summer after graduation was arguably worse than the preceding summer. By this point the ship had really sailed. There was no joining the party early: I had missed my chance and needed to figure something else out, and quick.

I huddled with my dad. I could sense he was waiting for me to come asking for help. To his credit, he had waited patiently as I fumbled around to figure out my path forward toward my dream. No doubt it gave him a little satisfaction when I asked him what he thought I should do next.

"Go work for Bill Clinton," he suggested. The president, a popular Democrat and a Southerner, was running for reelection, and he needed soldiers in the field.

I didn't hate the suggestion. I liked the president, respected his commonsense politics, and at this point in my story I was ready for something comfortable, more familiar. I had stuck my neck out long enough with only limited success. This would give me time to resume my cover while I figured out my next move.

My dad helped me connect with the campaign, and I jumped headlong back into state politics. I organized the campaign's presence throughout the state of Alabama. It was like riding a bike after a few years off. In other words, it didn't take long before I was flying. I assembled coalition and voter tables that were ready to get out the vote. I also organized an army of volunteers to knock on doors and pass out literature; we ran massive phone banks night after night to sway unpersuaded voters and ease concerns.

Oddly enough, I had a blast. I *loved* the energy of our team: everyone was hardworking, and we truly relished the late nights and the pizza and caffeine that came with it. It was fun to be good at something again, and it reminded me a little bit of playing a video game: I knew all the commands, and most times, I knew exactly what I needed to do. It reminded me of when I ran for student government in middle school and again in college. I could just see it.

The president won reelection, and before long I was back in Atlanta. A community service opportunity came my way, and in a snap decision I decided to take it. My spirits were up from the campaign, and I figured I could interview for jobs through a temp agency while doing something meaningful. The campaign reminded me of that essential truth: When in doubt, do something meaningful. Help somebody if you don't know how to help yourself. You'll find your way.

While I still didn't know what I was going to do, I was feeling a bit better about my place in the world. I started to believe once more that things would somehow work out. After some time away from Atlanta and the Morehouse bubble, I had a little more self-awareness. The end of my time at Morehouse had been hard. Turning down the conventional paths while my peers celebrated their offers at banks and big consultancies was hard to take. For a while, I'd gotten a little swept up in the whole who's doing what and where, and it unmoored me.

But now I was back in Atlanta, working at Dean Rusk Elementary School. A friend of my dad's, State Senator Horace Tate, introduced me to another legend in equity and education, Dr. Alonzo Crim. Dr. Crim was the first Black superintendent of Atlanta public schools and was a trailblazer in American education. He sent me to Dean Rusk knowing that it was a very tough school. He wanted me to understand—to truly understand—the link between education and equity. He wanted me to internalize the profound challenges many Black people encounter in the course of their everyday lives. I'll never forget, for example, learning on my first day at Dean Rusk that the average age of the grandparents of students enrolled in the school was thirty-six.

Thirty-six.

I was running Junior Achievement in the school, a program to teach business principles to the students. I was assigned to the third grade and fell in love with the kids. They were incredible. Curious, mischievous, playful, and so smart. Scary smart. And older than their years. When I looked into their eyes, I could see that they had seen too much, even at that tender age. Being with them hurt my heart and lifted my spirits at the same time.

There were other duties, too, of course. Most days, after school, some of the kids needed to be walked home. A student's mom or dad, or the adult guardian in their life, wouldn't show up, and all the teachers and educators would huddle to figure out who was taking who home. Invariably, one of the teachers would ask me, already knowing the answer: "Mr. Steven, can you walk them to the corner?"

I would take my kid up the street to where a group of older children, mostly teenagers, were milling about. One of them would volunteer to take the kid home to where they lived in the nearby housing projects across the street. What struck me was that Morehouse was *right there*, just a few blocks away from the projects, but for the Black boys at Dean Rusk, Morehouse might as well have been Mars.

I reflected on my journey. Education played such a huge role in my development, beginning in Montgomery. Now I had a world-class education from Morehouse. Hell, I was undecided about what to do next, career-wise, and I was back in the classroom, albeit as a teacher instead of a student. All my life, education was my saving grace. Why wasn't it for the children of Dean Rusk? It was a question that would haunt me for years after.

Outside of Dean Rusk, I continued to nurture my relationship with the temp agency. And in a few months I was placed at the MCI Communications Corp., a telecom company, at the time one of largest long-distance service providers in the country. I didn't *love* the work, but it steeped me in the guts of a large company where I could learn about corporate operations: a little marketing, some customer service, and lots of accounting. From day one, I knew MCI wasn't it for me, but the opportunity renewed my energy for my job search. I had a little momentum now, so I continued to press the temp agency, calling every day to see if they had a new opportunity for me.

And finally, one hot, sunny day, fortune smiled.

It started with a mix-up.

Professor Ben McLaurin had been a champion of mine since my junior year. As an officer with the Morehouse Business Association when my friend Dwight James was the president, he served as the faculty adviser. Professor McLaurin would inform me that there were great companies interviewing at the AUC Career Center and I should check it out.

When I made it to the career center, I was told that my interview had fallen through. They were interviewing candidates for American Airlines that day, and I was not supposed to interview for a role at the airline. I approached the woman running the career center and coordinating the interviews. She was middle-aged, with a professional demeanor, and she gave the impression that she took no nonsense.

"Hi, ma'am. My name is Steven Reed. I am a recent graduate. I am here to interview."

She peered at the sheet, looked up at me without expression, and peered back down at the sheet.

"There's been a mix-up. You aren't interviewing today. We're doing American Airlines."

"Do you think I could interview with American?" I asked, my voice earnest and maybe a little desperate.

"No, you may not," she said, somewhat offended by my suggestion. She looked up and peered at me over her glasses. Maybe she could sense my disappointment and more than a little bit of pain. I had been in the professional wilderness for a while. I was still lost.

"Well, actually," she offered, her tone a little softer, "someone did cancel. If you're back here in a couple hours, you can take their slot. But you'll need to wear a suit. A polo shirt and khakis won't cut it."

I broke out in a big smile, bouncing up and down in my shoes before extending my hand. "Thank you, ma'am. I'll be back here." She shook my hand before I hurried out. I didn't want her to change her mind.

As soon as I was out of sight, I was confused again. Did I even want to work for American Airlines? I called my brother, Joey.

Joey was working in law now. He was clocking serious billable hours. Every time we connected, he reminded me that time is money. "What's up, Steve? I've only got a minute."

"Hey, so what do you think of American Airlines?" I started.

"Flight benefits," Joey said, without missing a beat. "Some of my boys worked at Delta when we were in college. They liked it. Try it out."

That was all I needed to hear. I practically sprinted home, hit the shower, and changed into my best (and only) suit. When I made it back to the career center, they promptly called me back, where I met another woman who was warm and vibrant. We hit it off right away.

She graduated from the University of Michigan. I shared that my family in Detroit had always celebrated Michigan as a "public Ivy." It was a serious school that produced first-rate scholars every year. The biggest thing that came through was my curiosity and intense desire to do and be different. I had grown up in the traditional Deep South, had come of age at the impressive but conservative Morehouse, and was ready to break loose. I wasn't sure if I nailed every answer, but I gave myself an A for enthusiasm. They invited me out to interview at the corporate headquarters in Texas. And when I got the call to come out for the final interview, I felt my swagger starting to return. *Let's close this deal*, I said to myself after hanging up the phone.

I'll pause the story here. I *did* get my swagger back in that moment. But in the days and weeks before my lucky break I remembered something my dad had told me over and over and over when I was growing up:

"Keep God in the forefront. Pray and don't be embarrassed to ask people to pray for you, because you'll need it."

The truth is I was praying *a lot* during this time. Everything seems easier, almost inevitable, in retrospect, but while you're going through it, it's not easy or inevitable at all. Of all the times in my life, this was my wilderness. I knew I wanted more for myself and, more importantly, I wanted something different. But I didn't know how to get what I wanted.

It was humbling. I had a bit of a chip on my shoulder during my college years. On one level, I was tired of being shepherded along to follow the pack. To be honest, Morehouse steered you: if you were a political science major, then it demanded you be a lawyer. If you majored in finance or business, then it demanded you be an investment banker. From there, if you didn't work at a big law firm or on Wall Street, then you were made to feel you had underachieved.

On another level, I had a perception problem: "Oh, you're from the South?" *Then you must not be that smart.*

Or: "Oh, you play football? You're awfully small." *You must not be that good at the sport.*

I was tired—tired of feeling hemmed in by what others expected of me. I needed to live up to what I expected for myself.

The next few weeks were a whirlwind. Once I was in Texas, I raised my hand to participate in American's management leadership program. Few people my age opted to apply for the program, which was competitive, above and beyond American's standard hiring process.

I was hungry for the challenge and ready to engage with more experienced professionals.

I didn't want to go the way everybody else was going.

I was tired of being told what to do.

I was ready to break out.

Chapter 5

JOURNEYS

B efore I left for Morehouse, one of my dad's friends bluntly told me, "You need to major in business so you can learn more about how money works." His words stuck with me, and for four years at Morehouse I prepared for a career in business at a time when very few Black people operated at the top of American capitalism.

I learned the most from Dr. Belinda White, a marketing professor and the head of the Morehouse Business Association, the club in which I was most active throughout college. What Professor White taught me was that succeeding in business required more than head knowledge. So much of business success was about how you presented yourself. Whether it came to the workplace or a specific negotiation, she drilled into us the basics of professionalism.

Belinda White was on point. And more importantly, she took it as her sacred mission to make sure *we* were on point. She understood that, as Black men entering the workforce, we must find every advantage we could and avoid at all costs any foreseeable errors. She opened class with a lesson I never forgot.

"You are Black men," she began, "and you are discounted the instant you walk into the room. Therefore, when everyone else is good, you must be better. When everyone else is better, you must be the best. When everyone else is the best, you must be better than the best. All that starts with how you carry yourselves."

She taught us etiquette: how to dress; how to eat at a table; how to eat at a cocktail hour and balance your glass with a small plate full of food while still being able to shake hands; how to read *The Wall Street Journal*; how to read *Black Enterprise*; how to deliver an elevator pitch.

It all sounds so basic, but she was right. So much of life is about acting like you've been there before. And that starts with looking the part.

Professor White also drilled into us that "if you're going after internships, or a job, you're going to represent Morehouse. Remember, going in, you're Black. And you're likely going to be the first Black person in this internship program, and so you've got to be on point—with *everything*. Let's start with how you look. When you wear a suit, make sure it's navy, gray, or charcoal gray. No brown. And I'm sorry, but no black; in fact, here's a rule: no other Crayola color. Don't even think about wearing that."

And sure enough, in interview after interview for internships and jobs, those presentation factors made a huge difference. Some guys would show up looking like Jalen Rose, who wore a bright red suit as an NBA first-round draft pick, but with one critical difference: Jalen Rose is six-eight and the rest of us were five-eight. That look only works in the NBA.

I carried those lessons with me to American Airlines, my first real job after college.

When I showed up at Corporate HQ in Fort Worth, Texas, the first thing I observed was the emphasis the company placed on "respecting differences."

It was everywhere. On your name tag. On the walls. In your welcome packet.

At first, I scoffed a little bit.

Respecting differences? I grew up in Montgomery. Our city birthed the civil rights movement. We were the launching pad for Dr. Martin Luther King and Rosa Parks and the Civil Rights Act of 1964 and the Voting Rights Act of 1965. How many more differences are there left to respect?

It turns out, *a lot*.

American forced me to reflect on my experiences up to that point. Beginning with Morehouse, the sociocultural context in which I came of age was conservative. Morehouse men were a lot of things: serious, straitlaced, ambitious. They were also *heteronormative*. We had a handful of young men who identified as gay at Morehouse, but they weren't very open or loud about it, and our campus wasn't especially inviting to orientations that weren't heterosexual. Morehouse wasn't intolerant, but it wasn't affirming and encouraging of differences of orientation and sexual identity. It turns out, that's a big deal when you're eighteen, nineteen, and twenty. That climate, whether one realizes it or not, shapes you and the mores and expectations you carry with you throughout the world.

And it only took about five minutes at American to realize that there are more races and ethnicities across humanity than just Black and white. For someone raised in Montgomery, with its rich and all-consuming civil rights history, this was a shock to the system. First in Montgomery and then at Morehouse, my entire life experience until that point had been framed in the terms "Black" and "white." American was different. From my first day, the company was clear that it was a *global* company that served and hired from six continents: Asians, North and South Americans, Europeans, Australians, and Africans from the motherland all worked at the airline, and I met someone from each continent on my first day of work.

When our CEO addressed our incoming class of candidates in the management program, he led with something like this:

This company is about respecting differences—differences as people, differences of perspective, differences of identity.

We are a worldwide company and therefore we must have a worldwide focus. To succeed in a world as vast and diverse as ours, you must appreciate people who come from different backgrounds, different religions, different cultures—people who may not have the same exact experience as you do.

Here at American, you will work with gay people and straight people, Hindu and Muslim, Jewish and Catholic. You will work with everyone. *We are throwing you into the gumbo that is this organization, and at no point will you look around and say to yourself, 'This person doesn't belong here.' You are among the smartest, hardest-working, and most committed people you will ever meet or with whom you'll have a chance to work.*

We value diversity because it is our greatest strength. If you believe in freedom of expression, then you must also accept that having diversity at the decision-making table only leads to better results.

Ultimately, how you respect differences *will show us whether you're ready to stay and thrive here.*

I was awed. *Wow,* I thought. *These folks are serious about diversity.*

My time at American was transformative. I learned to work through the discomfort of diversity to achieve the promise of diversity, which usually meant better results, greater buy-in across stakeholders, and a shared sense that we were delivering solutions for everyone.

Working at the company instilled in me a global perspective that I carry with me to this day. For instance, one of the first things I did as mayor of Montgomery was to present a citywide nondiscrimination ordinance. In plain English, the ordinance meant Montgomery was taking a stand that we would affirmatively "respect differences."

What got lost in Montgomery at the height of the movement that they got right in Atlanta was the importance of respecting diversity. Atlanta, famously, is "the City Too Busy to Hate," as noted earlier. Across the decades, Atlanta's leaders didn't view diversity, equity, and inclusion as just something that's nice to have or even necessarily as a moral imperative. Rather, diversity, equity, and inclusion represented a *competitive advantage.*

How does that work? Well, the world is big. It's messy. It's complex. It's difficult. Valuing and fully leveraging diversity is essential to navigating our big, messy, complex, and difficult world. Fully leveraging diversity requires overcoming the discomfort of diversity to realize the promise of diversity.

I didn't learn that in Montgomery. I didn't learn that at Morehouse. I learned that at American.

I learned other things, too. I was initially deployed to the marketing department, where I worked with a global team to market to countries around the world. And there were so many products—not just flights. There was the Admirals Club. American Airlines Vacations. Credit cards and corporate retail partners. The AAdvantage Program (the first loyalty program of any airline). Food and beverage. And marketing was *powerful* at American: it was not just promotion but also fundamentally evaluating each business line for its profitability and return on investment.

The strongest performers on the marketing team could do two things. First, they could speak multiple languages and span more teams. I struggled here but did my best to keep up. And second, they centered the customer in everything they did. They always asked the question, "What is the customer experience, and how can we improve it?" Everything down to the kind of flatware included with the meals served on flights flowed from decisions in marketing. I internalized an attention to detail and a customer-centric orientation that guide me to this day.

When I started as the mayor, one of the first things I noticed about our city was that we didn't center the citizen in our public service. We didn't think about how the ordinary Montgomery resident experienced city services. How they "feel" government. Therefore, we didn't emphasize performance across city functions, from trash pickup to public safety to our schools. Good management is almost invisible. Things "just work." But bad management is painful and often obvious to anyone paying attention. In company cultures that are poorly managed, organizations often turn inward, away from the customer. They are consumed with small-*p* politics. Instead of being results oriented, a tendency to mediocrity takes hold across the workforce. Employees focus on "checking the box" instead of listening to the customer and working to solve their problem. These attributes overwhelm the system and drive out employees who are excellent contributors. It's a vicious cycle that, if left unaddressed, creates the culture of bureaucracy that many people hate about large companies that have become bloated or about government at all levels of our society. American taught me that the best organizations center people and create a culture that is performance driven and results oriented.

I also loved the level of innovation at American and the effort everyone invested in bringing that innovation to life. Innovation simply means finding new ways to solve old problems. At American, it was almost a game of one-upmanship. During an average week we worked seventy hours, trying to deliver the best results for our customers and pushing ourselves to find novel solutions to their problems. That level of investment was the norm. In a "good" week I might get away with working fifty-five or sixty hours, but usually it was seventy hours or bust. And once I joined the finance team, I didn't sleep, especially during budget season.

Working in finance at American trained me to be a rigorous, data-driven decision maker. Nobody cared what you thought until you crunched the numbers. Once the numbers were crunched, I was free to form an opinion and make my case, but we always had to root our decisions in evidence first. I also learned to work with multibillion-dollar budgets and appreciate the stakes behind numbers of that size. We quickly learned that people were affected by the numbers. If one decimal point was off, it could mean lost customers, delayed flights, or impacts on people's lives and livelihoods.

One of the best parts of the job, of course, was the travel. Joey nodded to this early on. Employees enjoyed great flight benefits to every corner of the world, which created a culture that was truly "work hard, play hard." Everyone would travel everywhere all the time. Sometimes it would be a weekend trip or a twenty-four-hour swing in a city, but the folks at American never stopped moving.

I made the most of this. I visited my friends from Morehouse who were spread across the country. I made new friends at the airline and traveled the world. Through it all, I kept in mind something that my dad had taught me when I was growing up: "Make new friends, but never leave an old friend in order to make a new one. Nothing is more painful than betrayal by a person who you believed was once your friend."

I was making a lot of new friends at American. And I didn't exactly leave Morehouse on the best of terms, but the more time that passed, the more I realized that that had more to do with me than with the people I was running with then. My college friends were great; that time of life was just hard. It felt good to be in a better place personally and to see my college friends in their element across the country. I'm glad I stayed close to my old friends and took care of them, and every day I am reminded of all the ways they've taken care of me, too.

And with my new friends at American, I traveled to parts of the Middle East, the Caribbean, Central America (including several parts of Mexico), and several countries in South America. I traveled to the Asian continent, touring Thailand and other parts of Southeast Asia.

My most impactful trip was to Bahia, which was once the largest slave port in Brazil.

As I looked over the bay that cuts into the coast of Brazil—the pale pink, green, and yellow stucco houses, the broad sugar plantations stretching farther inland—all the things that I read about in world history (the Middle Passage, the transatlantic slave trade, colonialism, the African Diaspora, imperialism) came to life. It hit me hard: race isn't just an American issue. They're grappling with it here in South America, too—hell, and worldwide. It's about power and domination and trade and commerce and conquest.

And just like we were struggling to build our city in our own image back in Montgomery, the indigenous Brazilians were still struggling to find their place in modern society. The trauma and the tragedy of the past weighed heavy on the people and the culture. It was beautiful and sad, just like home. I felt myself understanding home a little better, judging my people—my dad, in particular—a little less harshly for working so hard to make sense of their place in it. When I left for college, the civil rights work in Montgomery felt small. Now here I was halfway across the world, and suddenly it felt *so close*.

I had another realization in Brazil. While American Airlines was outstanding at "respecting differences," it wasn't perfect. In particular, the implicit bias of many of my white colleagues was very real and impacted the way they behaved in the workplace and interacted with their colleagues of color. For instance, a lot of white employees were fascinated with Europe above all else, and Europe was the only place they would go. Over drinks or meals or at the water cooler, they discouraged many of us from going to places where there were many people of color.

They would always caution or warn against going to most places outside of Europe that they considered too dangerous or risky. But when it was Europe, they encouraged us to go anywhere. It was pathological on some level and revealed a lack of true awareness or recognition of other people and cultures. It ultimately didn't impact my experience—I went to all those places anyway—but I grew more aware of the role that implicit bias can play in people and across a culture. And it revealed that just stating the best of intentions didn't overcome the dynamics of human nature at the company. Ultimately, people need to be responsible for their continued growth and self-awareness. We all have blind spots.

A lot of my white colleagues were uncomfortable being in places where they weren't in the majority. In contrast, when I traveled to a country with a majority Black or brown population, I had a fantastic experience: I made fast friends with folks, who quickly became like family. They would take me places and I never felt I was in danger.

I observed the same dynamic while traveling within the States. White colleagues would hype up certain cities and play down others. "St. Louis? Detroit? Memphis? Are you sure?" I never had much patience for that. I would often counter, "Man, my family, my folks, are in Detroit or Oakland. Y'all might want to go to San Francisco, but I am going to Oakland."

✳ ✳ ✳

I spent nearly five years at American Airlines. The experience changed my life. Personally and professionally, I transformed. By the time I was ready to leave for the next challenge, I was confident, battle-tested, and *clear*.

During my years at American, the siren song of entrepreneurship only grew louder. Working in an elite corporation, traveling the world, and performing under deadline with sophisticated, smart teams made me confident. But before I could build *my thing*, I needed a stronger network. Without it, I would struggle to raise the money and build the team essential to succeeding as an entrepreneur. Once I had the network, all I would need was a big idea and I would be ready to build.

My passion for Black wealth intensified and clarified. With my dad out of elected office, he had a little (just a little) more time for reflection. By the early 2000s, it was glaringly obvious that one of

Montgomery's biggest problems was its economy. Decades of segregation, white flight, and political gridlock that resulted from fighting Mr. Discrimination all but guaranteed that the city would stagnate.

Time and again, my dad and I would have the same conversation: "Dad, why didn't y'all think more about economics at the height of the movement? It seems obvious in retrospect. Thinking more selfishly, Dr. King *was poor*. In all that struggle, didn't you all want more for yourselves and for our people?"

"Well, we did think about money," he would counter. "Hell, Martin King got shot for marching for economic justice, not civil rights."

"I get that, but what about Black business, Black wealth, entrepreneurship—institutions we own and control that we can use to create opportunity for the community? What about that?" I asked.

My dad let out a deep sigh. He was tired. "Son, we focused on what we did so you can do what you do," he finished simply.

At the time, it wasn't a satisfying answer. It felt like a bit of a dodge. But I was older now, a full-fledged adult with real-world experience. I was ready to take on this challenge; I just needed a bit more training and a little investment.

I applied to several MBA programs. Business school made the most sense for me: it would serve as finishing school after my time at American, where I learned a lot but did not develop all the essential skill sets needed to run my own business. More importantly, I would grow a network that would allow me to access capital. Capital is the lifeblood of a business. Any child a few minutes into a game of Monopoly knows that. Cash is king. Without it, you're dead.

I needed to go somewhere top-flight. I wanted to be sure that the education truly deepened my knowledge of how capital markets worked and that the relationships I built there would follow me into my next endeavor. I landed on the Owen Graduate School of Management at Vanderbilt, a top school in the South with a stellar network behind it, in a city on the rise: Nashville.

Up until that point, I had never spent much time in Nashville. Always a quick hit now and then. So when I first made it to Nashville for graduate school, I observed two things right away.

First, the city even then was on fire: it was developing like crazy.

And second, it was very white.

Very white.

And I don't necessarily mean the population. Nashville was a majority white city, but its demographics weren't overwhelmingly white. About a fifth of the population was Black, and the immigrant community was exploding in size, tripling between 1990 and 2000.

But the culture that governed the place was white. When I walked into a hotel during my first visit to Owen, the receptionist, a Black woman, asked me what had brought me to Nashville. I started with "Well, I hear the music is really good," and before I could finish with something like "And I am thinking about going to school here," she guffawed. "Honey, you're in the wrong city for music. You need to shake your behind right up the street to Memphis." The implication was clear: this city wasn't necessarily designed for Black people.

Now, I like country music and don't agree with that assessment, but that was the feeling. More insidiously, though, it was almost as if the shop and store owners, restaurants, and bars weren't used to Black people coming inside and spending money. I always experienced a subtle sense of discomfort when I engaged with the locals. Like I was being watched. As if they were suspicious of *me*.

I didn't dwell on it, at least at first. I dug into my coursework at

Owen, and for the most part I enjoyed it. It was a serious program at a serious time: Enron had just gone under, and the emphasis on corporate ethics was at an all-time high. Business school is predicated on the case method coupled with a ton of group work, so it wasn't long before I was working with my classmates late at night and even early in the morning. We were turning around assignments, projects, and problem sets to keep up with our rigorous slate of classes.

I had learned a lot of things at American that helped me at Owen, but none were as foundational as the mantra "Work hard, play hard." That came in handy in Nashville, in particular.

The school was fantastic and the professors were great, but ultimately I was there for the network, so I threw myself into organizing one. As I had in Montgomery and at Morehouse and American Airlines, I expected to find an organized Black community in Nashville, but I was surprised to find that it was only loosely connected. And then I discovered the biggest shocker of all.

The club scene in Nashville is bad. Like, horrible.

Instead of clubs where you could dance, have a few drinks, and meet a boy or girl you fancied, Nashville was replete with opportunities to square dance. Let me say that another way. There weren't any nighttime spaces for Black folks. And that simply wasn't going to work. The lack of a nightlife and the subtle daytime racism that cut through the city's retail and restaurant scene added up to a reality in which Black folks steered clear of downtown altogether, which reinforced the sense that this place—this city—just wasn't for us.

I came to learn that it wasn't that Black folks weren't present in Nashville in a meaningful way—Black Nashville is very real—but there weren't spaces for us. That kept us from building a sense of community. On the other hand, white folks, fanatical about country music, had Bound'ry, the Trace, Sam's Place, and literally hundreds of other establishments where they could come together to enjoy one another.

But for Black folks, there wasn't a single venue, event, or club scene dedicated to us. We were frozen out.

This was a problem. I was there for a network, and I needed white *and* Black allies. Hell, from my time at American, I knew I needed friends from all over the world. We needed to draw from an established playbook to turn this around.

Enter Young Professionals Social, or YPS. YPS was modeled after "First Fridays," a Black networking tradition that had success in most major cities, especially those with large Black communities: Baltimore, DC, Atlanta, Chicago, Dallas—pretty much anyplace where there's a critical mass of brothers and sisters looking to congregate, connect, and socialize.

Through the years, a ton of professional associations like the Black Bar Association (lawyers), the Black Dental Association, Black MBAs, Black CPAs, and the like fueled the rise of events like First Fridays by co-opting the format for their version of regular networking. I saw an opportunity to do that in Nashville, and so, every month, I would bring together Black college graduates and young professionals—twenty-three and older, no undergrads—for drinks and a good time through YPS. We'd stake out a venue, buy out the bar, and make the place ours for the night. For six hours, it would be *our space*. Once a month was regular enough to establish a ritual but rare enough to sustain demand. There were enough expectations that it felt like going out to the club: a cover charge ($15), a dress code (no jeans, tennis shoes, or jerseys), and crowd control (someone at the door to make sure the vibe stayed right inside and didn't overwhelm).

Elegant: easy to get started and easy to scale.

Little did I know then that YPS would change my life. More on that later.

Like any start-up, our First Friday experiment started humbly enough: at Chili's.

That's right. Chili's.

I know what you're thinking. Chili's is *Chili's*. There's no vibe at Chili's. Why would a cool brother or sister step foot into a Chili's for Friday night fun? Well, first, under my watch, YPS transformed the Nashville Chili's from a sleepy bar and grill with just okay food and okay pours into the preeminent Black scene in all of Tennessee.

How? Well, when it comes to vibe, it was and remains all about the people.

The YPS vibe at Chili's was a cross between a family reunion and a nightclub. Folks hollering at each other from across the room, new connections and romances igniting, people trading laughs and stories—it was beautiful. It also drove home the fact that Black folks were hungry for an experience like this. Easily, on a given night, five hundred to nearly a thousand Black folks would pass through that Chili's. It was staggering. Chili's was making a small fortune off YPS, and after a few months it looked like the community we so desperately craved was coming together.

And then the music stopped.

One week, a few days before a YPS event, I swung by Chili's to make sure we were all set for Friday. The bartender, a white guy whom I had grown friendly with, greeted me with sad eyes.

"Hey, man, how are you feeling? We good for Friday?" I started, sidling up to the bar. The restaurant was basically empty except for a few waitstaff milling around, getting ready for the late-afternoon rush.

"I am okay, man. Listen, I've got bad news. Let me start by saying that we love you guys. Y'all come back in here anytime. But we can't do YPS anymore. We can't rent the space to you."

I was shocked. "We're spending hella money and you don't want it back?"

There was a long, awkward pause. Finally, he continued. "Well, it's just that ownership or management or whatever is trying to manage the perception of the establishment."

I chuckled. "Oh, so what you're basically saying is that YPS is too Black."

His faced turned scarlet. He shrugged and mumbled and looked down, wiping the counter. He was obviously embarrassed. Facts are facts. YPS was great for him and his colleagues—the tips were out of this world—and I believed we had established a genuine affection for each other during in our casual interactions. At every YPS, even the mostly white staff seemed to have a really good time. There was never any trouble, just revelry.

But ultimately, none of that mattered. Those in charge decided we had made the venue "too Black."

He continued to wipe the counter and wouldn't reestablish eye contact. Disgusted, I shook my head and muttered, "Dude, this is messed up." I pushed away from the bar and headed back outside.

This was clearly an injustice. And I am my father's son after all. I decided then and there, *this wouldn't stand*. My political organizing gene kicked in. My dad's voice reverberated in my head: "Some folks say politics is dirty. Politics is a noble profession. It's 'politricks' that's dirty."

Closing YPS wasn't politics: this wasn't a case of legitimate disagreement among competing stakeholders. This was *politricks*: racism, pure and simple. YPS was highly profitable, well attended, and safe. It should have been allowed to continue. Period.

I wrote an article for the *Nashville Scene* about the incident. It was published and the piece struck a nerve. The *Nashville Scene* is the alternative paper in Nashville, like *Creative Loafing* in Atlanta. I didn't just take aim at the fact that YPS, our only regular community space in Nashville, was shut down. I highlighted the subtle but undeniable racism of Nashville's retail and restaurant scene. I recalled how many Black people are followed while they shop for clothes or made to wait an unconscionably long time for service at a restaurant or bar. I emphasized how those microaggressions, however "small," created profound divides that held our community back from its enormous potential. And everyone knew it.

It was obvious to anyone who spent even a little time there that Jefferson Street divided Black Nashville from white Nashville, with neither side crossing into the other.

Those who went to Tennessee State didn't come over to Hillsborough Village or the West End, where Vanderbilt was located, and vice versa. And it didn't have to be that way.

Back at Owen, my classmates, white and Black, stepped up to come to my defense. Many, especially my white classmates, were shocked and asked me over and over, "This is what's really happening? In 2003?" I even had white friends who were graduates of West Point expressing solidarity. So many folks said, "Well, we'll come and support you guys." Together, we found a new venue, and they did come and support it.

The new YPS had med students from Meharry Medical College, white law students from Vanderbilt, business school students from Vanderbilt, Black undergraduate students from Vanderbilt, young professors who were working across all the local universities and colleges, and young professionals at local companies, ready to spend money.

It was great to have allies, and it was a powerful lesson in organizing. YPS created space for Black people—Black communion, Black celebration—but it was never intended to be exclusive. We didn't and still don't do what some white segregationists insist on doing to us. Our practice was never to turn someone away. We just wanted a space that welcomed and centered us and our experience.

Together, Black, white, and brown, we built it.

✳ ✳ ✳

So, how did First Fridays change my life?

While I was in graduate school, I continued a habit I'd picked up at American Airlines: I would visit friends in their cities around the country. I've always enjoyed moving around and I love seeing my people wherever they are. And my community really appreciates it. Coming from Montgomery, I knew what it felt like when no one ventured into my city. It's easy to overlook people and places that are, depending on who you are and where you're coming from, unfamiliar.

One weekend I made a jaunt down to Atlanta to visit some old friends from undergraduate school. I left early enough to catch the First Fridays there—which was well established and *lit*. A few of my friends had remarked that things had improved since undergrad. I had had many great nights at First Fridays as a Morehouse student, so I was curious to see how things had changed.

I came early and ordered a drink when I noticed a beautiful young woman about my age, sharply dressed, standing nearby. A friend of mine approached me and introduced us. Her name was Tamika. She was a law student. And, no, I could not have her number.

"You're going to regret it," I said with a big smile. "I will change your life."

She rolled her eyes.

She was beautiful. And smart. And grounded. She had grown up in New Orleans and, like me, left home for school. She wanted more for communities like the one she grew up in. I loved that she cared about people and the real issues facing them in their lives. For a period she had even pursued counseling as a profession. She wasn't afraid to get her hands dirty. We chatted for a few minutes more. I was instantly pulled in.

"You're sure I can't have your number?" I asked one last time, sensing that she was enjoying our conversation as much as I was.

"No, Steven"—she smiled again, her guard back up—"but it was nice talking to you."

Our mutual friend called later. "Hey, Steve," she said, "Tamika thought about it. She wants you to have her number." She read it out loud.

I laughed. "She must have had a better time than she let on."

"Well, she's intrigued," she answered.

Tamika and I have now been married for fifteen years. We have three beautiful children. There isn't a day that goes by when I am not profoundly grateful for her and our partnership. She keeps me in check and covers my blind spots. She's always the first to remind me *why* we serve: in the end it's all about people, and community.

And of course, in the end, Tamika changed *my* life.

Community—and having the space to build it—matters.

Chapter 6

HOMECOMING

M ike Tyson once said, "Everybody has a plan until they get punched in the mouth."

Leaving Montgomery for Morehouse was *the plan.*

Working at American Airlines, traveling the world while learning the craft of management, was *the plan.*

Going to Owen Graduate School of Management at Vanderbilt and acquiring a network and deeply meaningful relationships that have followed me since was *the plan.*

Coming home to Montgomery to start a business, only to fail spectacularly, well, that was *getting punched in the mouth.*

I can't pinpoint the precise moment when I decided that my first bid as an entrepreneur wasn't working out, but it was—spoiler alert—well *after* I stared down the barrel of an automatic pistol and was asked to hand over all the cash.

But before we get to that, let's start from the beginning.

When I graduated from Owen with my MBA, I knew it was "now or never" for a foray into entrepreneurship. After years of *talking* about it, it was time to take the leap. And I was ready. I had spent my formative years in Montgomery, Atlanta, Dallas, and Nashville—all great cities of the South. I knew those cities, and others just like them, as *markets.* I understood what customers and communities across the South wanted and, more importantly, demanded. As a region, the South is habitually overlooked for investment and new business creation. I was determined to reverse course.

At Morehouse and Vanderbilt, I built key relationships and acquired important head knowledge: marketing, finance, operations, business development. At American Airlines, I developed the work ethic and a results orientation that taught me to both get it done and get it done *right.* I was still young, but I was no longer immature. I was secure in myself and ready for the next challenge. I would return home to Montgomery and build a business.

Finding partners for business was easy. At business school, there were dozens of talented classmates whom I liked and respected and could envision working with on my upcoming business venture. But two individuals quickly came into focus.

First, there was James, my friend and classmate from junior high. After business school, we reconnected at a networking event. Ever since we were little kids, James absolutely killed it in school. I first picked up on his talent when we were in the seventh grade. James aced every test. He finished every assignment before anyone else. He was also a good dude. Need help on homework? Find James on the bus. He wasn't just smart; he was kind and generous.

After high school, James studied mechanical engineering at Auburn, which had a first-rate program. Afterward, he picked up another degree at Columbia before moving into IT in Atlanta. James had established himself and had the cash flow to help finance our start-up.

My other partner was my friend Chris, whom I also knew from junior high. Chris's strengths complemented mine. If I was the extroverted front man who nurtured relationships and (tried to) see around corners to anticipate what the business needed, Chris brought an abundance of technical skill and a strong grasp of business mechanics: Chris's native language was spreadsheets and pitch decks.

Finding the *right* business was harder. After a few false starts I landed on real estate. For most of my life I had been passionate about real estate.

I came by it honestly enough. My mom and dad built a modest real estate footprint over the span of decades. They held on to each home we lived in even as our growing family outgrew those homes. While my parents weren't wealthy by any means, their foresight meant security for our family. The residual income from each property helped finance our college educations. And the appreciation in value of each home would mean a safe, secure retirement for my parents when that time came. Their example taught me from an early age the power of real estate ownership as well as the responsibilities involved.

Most weekends growing up, I was in their rental house, helping my dad fix it up. When I was young, my job was to cut the grass or fix one of the pipes in the plumbing. As I got older, I provided more skilled labor. I would hang drywall, plaster ceilings, and install crown molding. As a result, I knew my way around with a hammer. I also had experience managing a property for tenants. I developed a strong sense of how to maintain a property for a family and how to work with them if their household lost a job or had a sudden financial setback. Helping my parents with their modest real estate portfolio amounted to running a business.

I kept up with the real estate trends throughout college and graduate school. I read all the industry magazines and attended as many conferences as I could. In the 1990s, I had the opportunity to hear Jesse Jackson speak about real estate development, technology start-ups (which were then largely concentrated in Silicon Valley), and high finance on Wall Street as the primary drivers of wealth in America. He pointed out that "coincidentally" these industries were the most inhospitable to Black people, and as result our people were poorly represented.

Morehouse drilled into me that our generation was the one to change all that. We would represent our people at the highest levels of industry.

That ambition never left me. Even as I worked right after college and when I went back to graduate school, I dreamed about working in real estate at a bigger scale. I imagined developing towers downtown and attracting companies that had long been missing from the South. Commercial real estate developers have the power to shape—and reshape—communities. After all, real estate isn't just about land; it's about the businesses on the land. A developer with a vision and a social conscience could chart an entirely different course for a city or even an entire region.

As I finished graduate school and watched Nashville embrace its renaissance, it became clear to me that if a city like Montgomery was ever going to reinvent itself, it needed better leaders in real estate who intimately understood Montgomery's hidden strengths and opportunities. *There* was the opportunity.

To me, it was obvious: after years in the wilderness, Montgomery was finally turning into a tourist destination. The city's civil rights history attracted hundreds of thousands of people every year. We brought in tourism but we weren't making the most of that economic opportunity. The city was underdeveloped. We needed services, better food choices, and more amenities. We needed to remake the city into a destination that was family-friendly and inexpensive.

I envisioned bringing franchises into Montgomery that would serve the families who ventured into the city for the day or even an afternoon. A successful franchise did two things: it contributed a valuable service to the community and created value in the underlying real estate. *This* was how I was going to win in real estate.

My dad, of course, hated the idea.

"You should think about politics instead, son. You're a natural," my dad told me in between bites of a cheeseburger one afternoon at lunch. "And besides, with franchises, you'll be in the restaurant business much more than the real estate business. Too much headache for thin margins."

"Dad, with all these families coming into the city to learn about what your generation did to remake this country, they need better options. All we've got are greasy spoons. I love these cheeseburgers, but this joint isn't exactly a destination."

"How much was your cheeseburger?" my dad grumbled, his mouth stuffed full of fries.

"What?" I asked. I couldn't make out what he was saying.

"How much was your cheeseburger?" he asked again after swallowing.

"Two dollars."

"Exactly. *Thin* margins."

I didn't listen.

Unlike a lot of cities in the Northeast, the Mid-Atlantic states, or even the Midwest, the franchise explosion had not arrived in Montgomery yet. There was a bias against the South. A lot of national chains regarded communities like Montgomery as either too small or lacking a future bright enough in which to invest.

With James's initial investment, Chris's hard skills, and my relationships, we could put Montgomery on the map.

Our plan was simple: identify a promising franchise, bring it to Montgomery, and, assuming success, scale our footprint by bringing other franchises into the city. Once we reached a certain size, we would have enough cash flow and access to financing to enter other markets in the South. If everything went according to plan, we could run a multimillion-dollar venture within five years.

First, we needed to find a franchise partner who shared our passion for building in and developing the South. This was important. Pleading with a partner who didn't want to invest in the region wasn't worth our time. It turns out, we didn't need to look far. The Roly Poly sandwich shop in Birmingham was a regional franchise that, by the early aughts, had become one of the fastest-growing chains in the country. Its roots on the East Coast gave us comfort that we could scale fast in the South if we proved that the demand— and therefore the profits—were there.

When we met with Roly Poly, they were excited. They loved our team and our focus on Montgomery as a first market, and they understood and believed in our vision.

But there was one catch.

The franchise needed to be owner operated. At least the first shop. That meant that at least one of us needed to personally operate the franchise. That meant opening and closing the shop, managing inventory, supervising employees. The three of us huddled. If we were building our initial presence in Montgomery, then I was the natural—read *only*—option as operator. James was out. He lived in Atlanta and was clear from the beginning that he wasn't going to move. And Chris wasn't living in Montgomery: it would take him too long to commute to build the trust and the local network to operate effectively.

I wanted this. And I believed in our vision. I didn't love the idea of running a sandwich shop—in fact, there were few things I could imagine liking less—but our plan and our path had led us to this moment. It was now or never.

I said yes. And with dizzying speed I now owned and operated a sandwich shop.

As I watched the team from corporate affix the signage to the front of our small building in Montgomery, I thought, *How hard could it be?*

Remember what Mike Tyson said? Well, running this sandwich shop was like getting punched in the face. Every day.

I discovered that, in the world of small business, something is always going wrong. And there's no small business as difficult as the restaurant business. The margins on a sandwich, calculated according to the cost of goods sold, were, as my dad predicted, painfully thin. And while James had some cash flow to help us acquire the license to franchise, we didn't have sufficient capital to plow into the business until we were profitable. This proved decisive in the unsustainability of the business.

Early on, I went to all the local banks. Our fledgling business needed investment or, at a minimum, a line of credit to finance regular expenses: payroll, payments to suppliers and contractors, the mortgage. I thought investing in or financing our business was a no-brainer. After years of decline, Montgomery was beginning to rediscover itself as an important, historic destination. We needed businesses just like ours to contribute to the city's culture and vibrancy.

But we heard the same thing over and over and over.

"I am sorry, but you don't have enough personal assets to guarantee the debt."

"I am sorry, but the business has no track record. There's no record to loan against."

"I am sorry, but the business just doesn't generate enough returns to justify the opportunity costs. I understand what it does for the community, but Montgomery isn't vibrant enough to make this business a 'home run.' I can simply make more money investing elsewhere."

It was a catch-22. Because I was young, with only modest savings to my name, the banks wouldn't lend. Because our business was new, the banks wouldn't lend. Because our business was headquartered in a community that really needed us, the investors wouldn't invest because our city *wasn't* Nashville or Atlanta, where they could make more money from franchises.

No matter where I turned, the answer was no.

Something else was going on, too. I had only modest savings because my family was just a few generations removed from a time when *we* were the wealth. In just a few short decades my parents cobbled together a dignified life and retirement for themselves while sending their children to college. For me as well as for my brother and sister, our human capital signified our net worth. Our achievements represented a remarkable distance traveled by our family—one that spanned generations. A hundred years ago, my grandparents tilled the soil just as their grandparents had done as enslaved people. My parents sacrificed everything to change the laws so that their children—me, my brother, and my sister—could pursue our full measure of happiness in America.

Fast-forward, and between the three of us business partners, we have three college degrees, two master's degrees, and an MBA, and yet we don't qualify for a modest line of credit to accelerate a needed business because we "don't have a track record."

As mayor, one of the things I am most proud of is all the work we've done to make our city friendlier and more supportive of Black-owned small business. We've poured millions of dollars into loan funds that take chances on Main Street entrepreneurs. Those loan funds recognize that Black people have not had access to capital for generations, and as a result, we've been denied the opportunity to build wealth and necessary creditworthiness. Without bold investments like these from our public sector, there's nothing in the private markets to correct the chicken-and-egg problem I encountered as a young Black entrepreneur trying to build a business in my hometown.

Our inability to raise capital was a harsh wake-up call early on in our business venture. We were going to have to build the business the old-fashioned way: we would bootstrap it and grow it with free cash flow that the business earned. One sandwich at a time.

Practically speaking, that meant making sandwiches and thinking about how to sell sandwiches, 24/7. I wish I was exaggerating. For damn near four years I spent every waking minute in that sandwich shop or thinking about that sandwich shop: crunching numbers, running payroll, trying to schedule and cover shifts, pleading with people to stay for a few more weeks instead of leaving for another job or school, and begging people just to come to work. The life of a small business owner is relentless.

And the consequences of our lack of capital showed up everywhere.

For starters, we were chronically short-staffed. I ended up covering a lot of shifts. We couldn't pay for talent, and consequently, we attracted a lot of young people who were, to be fair to them, in a transient period of their life. Maybe they were working through college, or maybe they were working while on a break from college, or maybe this was just the thing they were doing *this week*, but next week they were on to something else.

I broke up a lot of fights and disagreements, too. It's hard to work and survive on minimum wage, and while those kinds of jobs are usually short-term assignments for people as they make their way through school or climb the career ladder, for many people it's the only thing that's available to them. Whether someone was working in our shop for a season of their life or the job was their life, it almost always meant that their life was hard and challenging. Maybe they had kids at home or they were helping their parents pay the bills. It was a lot of hard work for not a lot of money. Sometimes tempers ran out and fists would fly.

I learned that part of my job was coaching and developing everyone who worked for me and, most importantly, I wanted to leave everyone who worked at our shop better off than when they first came. Sometimes that meant helping my employees work on their soft skills, like how they dressed or presented themselves. (I would channel Belinda White.) Other times that meant working with them on their hard skills, like their math at the register. It always meant taking an interest in other people in the workplace. It wasn't always easy, but I loved that part of the job.

Because I covered so many shifts, I made a lot of sandwiches. Easily, thousands of sandwiches. The secret to a good sub? Thinly slice *everything*. The only thing thinner than our margins were our ingredients: iceberg lettuce, tomatoes, onion, ham, salami, and cheese. All sliced razor thin, laid on a loaf of bread that's crunchy on the outside and soft on the inside. Season with a little salt and pepper, red vinegar, dried oregano, mayo, and mustard. That's it.

I constantly battled with contractors and suppliers. We couldn't afford to pay top dollar—hell, we couldn't afford to even go middle of the road—so we often had to go the *discount* route. Unsurprisingly, the service was often bad. When a contractor or a supplier didn't honor the contract, we'd hassle and haggle until we would come to new terms. And until it got worked out, their jobs became my job.

And those jobs were *dirty jobs*.

Once, our janitorial contractor just stopped showing up. Of course, we refused to remit payment when they demanded it. Why would we pay when they weren't doing the work? A principled stand, for sure, but one that brought me down on my hands and knees to scrub bathroom floors and public toilets every morning and every night for months.

Another contractor never fully emptied our dumpster. That was not just shoddy work: the trash was building up inside the container week after week as a result. It was starting to become a problem, and I was worried it would begin to attract vermin and other critters if we didn't deal with it soon. And *that* would spell certain death for our fledgling restaurant. So one night I was headlong inside the container, pulling out months'-old garbage bags and waste. One of my employees, a young kid who went by the nickname "Terrence"— his real name was Charles—was standing behind me, one hand on his nose and another holding a bigger garbage bag.

Terrence was a lot of fun to work with and the self-appointed class clown. He was a seventeen-year-old kid working for the summer to make some money for his car. His car was always breaking down and it was always short of gas. Come to think of it, while I heard a lot about the car, I never actually laid eyes on it. Actually, I am not even sure if Terrence had a car. I figure he was trying to get his money right so he could get his ride right.

Anyway, Terrence reminded me of me, at least when I was younger. He had a response ready for every question or prompt, even—or especially—when he didn't know what he was talking about. Terrence was good at *making you think he got it*, but he never got it. If you asked him to take out the trash, invariably a bag would break open and spill out onto the floor. If you asked him to make a sandwich for a customer, he would leave a key ingredient off because he was distracted. Or he would incorrectly count the change.

With Terrence, it was always something. But that's being seventeen. Nevertheless, he was charming, confident, and more than a little silly, and he was, fundamentally, a good person. Young, trying to figure it out—just like the rest of us.

One night I was out front, wiping the counters before closing. Terrence stood behind me, twirling a broom like it was a martial art *bokken*. It was 9:57 p.m. I closed my eyes as I cleaned, I was exhausted. We closed at ten. Just a few minutes left.

I never closed early, for two reasons. First, there was almost always someone racing through the door right before we closed, desperate for a sandwich. I was convinced that serving those individuals created loyal customers. We couldn't afford not to convert a single loyalist. And second, we weren't just building a business: we were establishing a presence in the community and therefore a reputation. If our new shop closed early, it would signal to everyone that we weren't serious about our success.

At that moment the door burst open. *Probably a student jonesing for a sandwich,* I thought to myself as I wiped the counter, taking in the scent of ammonia. When I lifted my eyes, I was met with the barrel of a gun.

"Give me all of the money!" a man with a mask roared. The gun trembled ever so slightly, just inches from my face.

I froze, and the blood drained from my face as I stared down the barrel. My first thought was piercingly clear: *Man, what am I going to tell Terrence's mom if this guy kills him?*

And then another thought: *I've just got to get him out of here.*

My mental reflexes kicked in. "Listen, man, I'll give you all the money. Just don't shoot anyone. I am going to reach for the money. You can have all of it."

Out of the corner of my eye, I could make out Terrence's shocked face. He had dropped the broom and stood there, mouth agape, his body frozen with fear. As I pulled the money out of the register, never taking my eye off the gun, I slowly shifted my body to the right. I wanted to stand between Terrence and the would-be shooter. With one hand up to signal defense and another hand working its way slowly into the register, I pulled out the cash.

As I cleared the register, I felt a pit in my stomach. We did not do a midday run that day. There was a lot of money in the register. This was rare. Usually, we had enough staff on-site that I could leave the shop and deposit our cash at the bank during business hours. That was best practice. After all, businesses with little to no cash on hand aren't targets for robberies.

But today was different. All day, it had been just me and Terrence. No time to empty the register for a run to the bank.

We always trained our cashiers to give the money, without complaint or resistance, to anyone demanding it. In the end, protecting human life was supreme. No amount of money was worth jeopardizing lives over. This time would be no different.

The man with the gun stalked in front of me; he was waving his gun now. He was impatient and agitated. *Man, I cannot let anything happen to this kid back here,* my mind screamed.

"Sir, settle down. I've got all your cash right here. No one is going to stop you from leaving with it."

"Just put the money in the bag!" he yelled. I shoved handfuls of cash into the bag while he waved the gun. I was now squarely in front of Terrence. If the worst happened, he would have a few critical seconds to bolt to safety.

After what felt like an eternity, I put all the money into the bag. The register was completely empty.

"Is there any more money?"

"No, this is it. Please, just leave."

The man maintained eye contact for one more moment. I could see the wheels turning in his mind as he debated whether or not to pull the trigger. And then, in an instant, he turned and fled out the front door. He jumped into a getaway car that waited out front before speeding off. Terrence was still frozen with shock. The clock turned to 10:00 p.m. I hurried to the front door to lock it before calling the police. My heart was pounding so hard, it felt like it was going to leap right out of my chest. I could hear my heart thumping in my ears.

One thought turned, over and over, in my head: *We are alive. We are alive. WE ARE ALIVE.*

✳ ✳ ✳

After the burglary, I soldiered on. At least for a while. More late nights, more early mornings. Opening and closing the shop. Slicing sandwich ingredients thinner and thinner. But in the end it was math. The margins just weren't there. No matter how efficiently we ran our operation, the business didn't have the customer volume, nor could it sustain the higher prices needed to turn a meaningful profit. Without profitable margins, there wasn't enough money left over to invest in the marketing and promotion that would grow the top line of the business. Without growth, our first franchise was most likely our last. And on this business alone, I couldn't sustain myself or my family. We were barely getting by.

What was most frustrating was that, despite four years of

successful operation, the banks and investors never changed their tunes.

"I am sorry, Mr. Reed, we just don't lend to restaurants."

"I am sorry, sir, but your personal collateral is insufficient to secure the loan."

"I admire what you're trying to build in Montgomery, but we can make more profits in Atlanta. I am sorry, but we must deploy our dollars elsewhere."

I *knew* the entrepreneurial pathway was hard, but I didn't know it would be *this* hard. Our inability to raise capital made it almost impossible to build a business from the ground up in Montgomery. Sure, Montgomery needed goods and services to compete in the global economy; it needed amenities to attract tourists and keep young professionals in the city, just like every other major American market. And while our future demanded it, and investing in entrepreneurship was the only path there, our local ecosystem was wholly unprepared when it came to supporting business in the Black community. The banks wouldn't lend, the investors wouldn't invest, and our public leaders, meanwhile, sat back and watched while they bemoaned the city's lack of dynamism.

After four years of working my heart out, and with little to show, it was painfully clear: the next leg of the civil rights movement still needed to be run. We had to finish what Dr. King had started at the very end of his life: leveling the playing field of our economic system.

Another thing was painfully clear: my life and priorities had changed. I was no longer, as they say across the South, "bright-eyed and bushy-tailed." I now had a wife and a daughter. We had bills and growing obligations. After four years I could no longer afford to bring home only a pittance. I was frustrated that all my education hadn't led to more financial success. It was time for a change.

I didn't know what was next, but I knew I wasn't done with business. At least, not yet. *This* business didn't work, but in my heart I sensed there might be another path—one that would help people, first, and help reshape the very ecosystem in which we were building.

I needed time to figure it out.

So I started to shut down the sandwich shop. We had failed. It was time to move on.

In the meantime, Tamika and I settled into our lives in Montgomery. We didn't have much financially, but those were happy days. Even though my professional direction was unclear, I felt settled. Coming home to a family of my own shifted my sense of self in the world. It pulled me out of my own ego. My preoccupations shifted away from making money, or gaining notoriety as a successful business leader, to something both slower and truer: family, friends, faith, and a life devoted to helping others.

I didn't recognize it then, but my path to public service started that night at 9:57 p.m.

Chapter 7

EPIPHANY

In 2007, I made my way down to Selma, Alabama, which is near where my mother grew up, to attend service at Brown Chapel AME Church. It was a special day because United States senator and presidential candidate Barack Obama was making an appearance.

In 2007 the senator was crisscrossing the country to wage what would be a historic and successful bid for the White House. I followed Senator Obama from afar. Unlike some of the other rising stars in the party, Senator Obama didn't come up in the South or through the networks of faith or HBCUs with which I was familiar. So I was curious to learn more about him.

Specifically, I wanted to understand what experiences had forged him. Just five minutes into the senator's talk, it was clear that he was not only one of us—he was among the best of us.

Just like members of my mom's family, the senator found his purpose in the South Side communities of Chicago, where he started his career in faith-based organizing. Through a network of churches, Obama organized and strengthened the community by providing literacy programs, job training, and leadership development programs for community members.

Through the years, the senator turned down increasingly lucrative opportunities in Big Law and cushy, well-compensated foundation jobs to stay close to the community he had dedicated his life to serve. He was the real deal.

It wasn't always a smooth road for the senator. By his own admission, he got his butt whooped by Bobby Rush, a veteran South Side politician of my dad's generation, in a race for Congress. But he didn't let that discourage him. He stuck with public service, through its many ups and downs, and forged a life and career rooted in meaning. He changed things for people. And the more he succeeded, the more positions of responsibility he was entrusted with: state senator, United States senator, and now presidential candidate.

Obama's speech that spring morning was a beautiful sermon: a meditation on service, reflecting on those who had served before us, the Moses Generation, and those called to serve today, the Joshua Generation.

Obama reminded us that the Moses Generation, including my uncle, who had served in the segregated armed forces and was a member of the Brown Chapel AME choir, was still with us. And those of us who follow them, in life and leadership, stand on the shoulders of giants because they battled "not just on behalf of African Americans but on behalf of all Americans; they battled for America's soul, they shed blood, they endured taunts and torment and, in some cases, gave the full measure of their devotion."

That last part, of course, refers to those like Dr. King, Malcolm X, Medgar Evers, Robert Kennedy, Viola Liuzzo, James Chaney, Andrew Goodman, and Michael Schwerner—and countless others— who gave their lives to the cause. Death is so present in the fight for civil rights, across all American history, that it's easy to carry it lightly. Obama's poetry and the gravity of his pursuit for the presidency gave new weight to that sacrifice. I felt heavy.

Obama connected the work of the Moses Generation, and their long march through the desert, to the opportunities and advantages enjoyed by my generation. That law school education, the outstanding college experience, and a community of Black *and* white people who rooted for our success and largely cheered us on in every endeavor.

He shouted out other civil rights greats—Anna Cooper and Marie Foster and Jimmy Lee Jackson and C. T. Vivian, the Reverend Joseph Lowery, John Lewis—and asked us to sit with the cost of it all: cracked skulls and innumerable indignities suffered so that a Black kid with a funny name could sit and serve in the United States Senate.

Obama then spoke to our generation, the Joshua Generation. It was an unmistakable call to action that was rooted in gratitude and, indeed, a palpable sense of indebtedness. "I'm here because somebody marched. I'm here because you all sacrificed for me." And he reminded us that the job was unfinished. "I thank the Moses generation; but we've got to remember, now, that Joshua still had a job to do . . . We're going to leave it to the Joshua generation to make sure it happens. There are still battles that need to be fought; some rivers that need to be crossed. Like Moses, the task was passed on to those who might not have been as deserving, might not have been as courageous, find themselves in front of the risks that their parents and grandparents and great-grandparents had taken. That doesn't mean that they don't still have a burden to shoulder, that they don't have some responsibilities. The previous generation, the Moses Generation, pointed the way."

And then there was a moment when Senator Obama seemed to speak directly to me.

There is a certain poverty of ambition involved in simply striving just for money. Materialism alone will not fulfill the possibilities of your existence. You have to fill that with something else. You have to fill it with the golden rule. You've got to fill it with thinking about others. And if we know our history, then we will understand that that is the highest mark of service.

Listening to Obama, in that moment I suddenly felt self-conscious and a little bit ashamed.

For years I had been consumed with making money. It started innocently enough. As a kid, I was obsessed with increasing the level of Black wealth in our community. But over time my ambition had curdled into a desire to make as much money as possible *for me.* At the sandwich shop, I sliced the vegetables and the meats thinner and thinner, trying desperately to save a few cents that I could use elsewhere to grow the business. I needed it to work.

Now, when faced with *any* opportunity, I would ask myself, *How much money is this going to make me?* That's a fair question with which to start. But it's a problem if the questions stop there. As Obama said that morning, the right question is: *What will this opportunity do for others?*

After Obama's sermon, I stumbled out of the church and into the blinding afternoon light. Senator Obama's words played and replayed in my mind: "There is a certain poverty of ambition involved in simply striving just for money. Materialism alone will not fulfill the possibilities of your existence."

By the time I made it home, I knew what I needed to do. I still believed in business as a lever of change, but the franchise business wasn't it. I needed to build a business that had a purpose at its center. A purpose greater than just me.

The purpose was obvious. My failure in business was partly the result of a system that wasn't rooting for my success. We couldn't access the capital we needed to scale the business. Navigating government, to acquire the necessary permits or take advantage of some of the grant programs meant to bridge the capital divide, was virtually impossible unless you knew someone on the inside. Worse yet, our education system struggled to produce the educated workers we needed to hire to carry out the business. Some organs of government specialized in connecting small business owners to qualified local talent, but again, unless you knew someone, it was difficult to get connected.

As I immersed myself in the Montgomery business scene, I discovered I wasn't alone. There were *so many* other Black entrepreneurs who were experiencing the same challenges. I discovered a problem I believed I could help solve: helping other small businesses, especially Black-owned businesses, access the capital and strategic relationships they needed to succeed. For too long, the powerful halls of Montgomery—from the banks to the Capitol—were closed to people who looked like me. That needed to change.

Interestingly, this business went far better than my adventure in the restaurant industry. I learned that leadership could overcome any practical deficiencies in the business. My government affairs shop was small, scrappy, and lacked the same access to capital as the sandwich shop. But the government affairs shop had a purpose and a righteous cause at its center, which empowered me to lead. We had far more success, far more quickly, than when I was selling sandwiches. I didn't have a bigger purpose at Roly Poly. (Not to take anything away from food entrepreneurs, but selling food wasn't my calling.) Back then, I was just focused on making money.

It was healing to help other entrepreneurs in their journey. Maybe all those sandwiches were not for nothing. During this time, my dad was a huge help, too. He never said it out loud, but I could tell that he was very pleased that I'd come home to Montgomery. And even if I hadn't gone into politics per se, I was broadly helping our community improve. We talked, *really talked*, for what felt like the first time in years. We were no longer talking past each other. I could see that our worldviews had started to converge. He agreed with me that we needed to prioritize economic development in the Black community. I agreed with him that racial discrimination and segregation remained the biggest forces working against Black people in Alabama.

My mother was instrumental during this time as well. The regular family meals, the probing conversations, and our regular check-ins resumed as if nothing had ever changed. We established a cadence, a rhythm, to our lives. Mom was over the moon that I was home: she was excited to see her grandchildren raised in the same city that raised me and my siblings.

My parents agreed with me that teenagers are difficult to raise. They affirmed that sometimes children can be hurtful. I was raising a daughter who was growing into a teenager, and I could see through her eyes that, as her dad, I'd gone from knowing everything when she was a small child to knowing nothing in the span of just a few short years. It was obviously a phase, a natural part of life and growing up. But it didn't hurt any less.

I thought about some of things I had said to my dad when I was her age, and I had to admit that I had discounted a lot of his important, hard work. My dad is a member of the Moses Generation that then Senator Obama referenced, the very generation that made it possible for my generation to do what we do—from business to politics to sports to entertainment. But without giants like my dad, where would we be?

It was healing to reconnect with him, and I was fired up to tackle a new challenge.

From that time, I remember Miss Sophia, of Sophia's BBQ, a Black business owner who was trying to get a permit to expand her food truck, a fledgling soul food restaurant that served incredible smoked ribs, creamy mac and cheese, and fresh collard greens. Everyone knew Miss Sophia made the best ribs in Alabama, and folks would come from all over to eat them. The sauce was just the right amount of sticky, sweet, and smoky. But Miss Sophia's permit was stuck in the process. She had engaged another public relations firm, one without much of a track record. They were building their book of business and said yes to every client, whether or not they could help them. Miss Sophia spent a small fortune trying to get the permit done, with no success. I took her on, at no cost, because it was the right thing to do. She needed help, and I believed I could make a difference.

Miss Sophia's experience reminded me of something my dad had said all the time when I was growing up. "Keep in mind that you can't send for your lunch by way of a hungry boy. He'll eat it! Leaders who are hungry are greedy. They'll let their stomachs prevail over their principles."

I wish I could say Miss Sophia's experience was uncommon, but, honestly, it wasn't. I was helping as many people like her as I could, but even that started to feel a bit like Whac-A-Mole. By the time I fixed one issue for one client, there was another client frustrated by the same exclusionary system, calling for help. There were too many "hungry boys" profiting off the exclusion of good, honest, hardworking people like Miss Sophia.

I realized that my experience at Roly Poly wasn't anomalous. Too many good people in the city were confronting the same roadblocks. That realization began to radicalize me in the direction of politics. I got fed up with the mediocrity and indifference that characterized too many of our elected officials throughout the state. We needed change, and fast.

So I begged *my friends* to run. I urged *friends of friends* to run. In fact, I started making new friends just so I could ask *them* to run.

Wanted: smart, homegrown community leader hell-bent on creating a new Montgomery.

But all of them said no.

I heard every excuse in the book.

"Politics is dirty."

"Even if I got elected, nothing would ever change."

"The system's broken beyond repair."

"I can't afford to stop what I am doing to run for office."

"No one would vote for me anyway."

One day I was pushing a friend, Vernetta Perkins, a local leader, to think about a run for the school board, when she turned the question right back to me. "Steven, you're out here trying to convince me to run—why don't *you* run for office?" I was taken aback by her question and unprepared to answer. Before I knew it, I was providing the exact same excuses that I had heard, and detested, for months.

I raised that conversation with my dad, who didn't miss a beat. He highlighted that my experiences as an entrepreneur and my expertise in breaking down barriers for small business owners were a good fit for probate judge, the county official who approves the permits for people like Miss Sophia. "Well, don't you have to be an attorney to be a probate judge?" I countered. Before my dad could respond, I countered that he talk to my brother, Joey, an attorney, instead.

My dad was unmoved. He pointed out that Alabama's old, outdated constitution says you *didn't* need a law degree to serve in the role. The seat was currently held by a Republican, Reese McKinney, who had been in the job since the late 1990s. Reese was old-school. He was a creature of the system, working his way through various administrative roles before settling into the role of probate judge. Furthermore, there had never been a Black person elected to the role. Not only would I have to upset a long-standing Republican incumbent, but I'd have to break the racial barrier, too.

From the outside, at least, it seemed like Reese did not run the office well: it was slow-moving, bureaucratic, comfortable. There was little incentive to change because the longer a civil servant or elected official was in a role, the more power with which they were entrusted. Increasing efficiency and producing results were not rewarded. If the probate office was going to change, we would need a leader who could drive and manage change. A whole lot of innovation and analytical rigor was needed to break through the red tape and make the office function well for all Alabamians. Reese might have been a competent jurist, but in the end, that was a small part of the job. The probate judge first and foremost needed to know how to run things, especially how to move business permits, wills, marriages—indeed the laws that order our lives—to make people's lives better.

The more I batted around the idea, the more I liked it. I could run, serve a term, clean up and reform the probate office, and make life easier for a generation of entrepreneurs. People like Miss Sophia. After serving, I would transition back to the private sector. Unlike a lot of folks who run for office or get involved in government, I was not obsessed, then or now, with longevity in public life. Election and reelection are job interviews. And throughout my life, I've seen that if you're doing a good job, then the interview usually takes care of itself. And if it doesn't, then it isn't meant to be.

It helped that my dad was encouraging. He believed I could win because I brought something different to Montgomery: a new energy and, more importantly, a new perspective. "The city's ready to turn the page, son. Be true to yourself and stand tall. They'll be with you."

That felt right. A little scary, too: standing tall and all, because in politics there's always risk that the people *won't* be with you. You take too many difficult positions and suddenly you find yourself out in the cold—without support and vulnerable to challenge. As such, too many folks in politics orient their careers around staying in office at all costs—even at the cost of doing a good job. In the end, I never subscribed to that notion. My view is more in line with the nation's founding idea of public service: it is an honorable calling to answer, but those in power should never cling too tightly to it because it must be continually earned. Ultimately, it's up to the people to decide who will govern. Those of us fortunate enough to serve should focus on doing that well.

To prepare for the campaign, I studied like I was back at Morehouse. I surrounded myself with legal advisers and boned up on wills, estates, and probate law. If I was going to run, I wanted to give it my all—leave it all on the field.

The prospect of running a campaign reminded me of starting a business. So much of it is living with uncertainty and "controlling the controllables"; that begins with executing your plan. Most important is being one of the first out of the gate: either you set the terms of the race or someone else does it for you. Even *that* doesn't guarantee success. In politics, like life, anything can happen. Again, to quote Mike Tyson: "Everybody has a plan until they get punched in the mouth."

This time I was determined to do the punching.

✳ ✳ ✳

Deciding to run was one thing. Running *and* winning was another.

When I announced my campaign for probate judge, my first for public office, there was a significant number of people who questioned whether I was the right person to run, while others doubted my ability to win. The incumbent was someone who was viewed in many quarters as "one of the good ones" even though he was part of a party and an establishment that hadn't changed much in Montgomery for decades.

For some voters, there were deeper questions, and an abiding skepticism, too. Among some white voters, there were questions about the competence of Black officials in elected office. Among some Black voters, there was fear of retaliation if a significant segment of the community voted for a candidate other than the incumbent and that alternative candidate *didn't* win. "Then what?" many asked fearfully in the quiet of their homes.

And, of course, there were the inevitable comparisons to my dad.

"This will just give the Reeds too much power."

"Steven is a carbon copy of his father, so we can't expect any different *or* better."

Others counseled, "Wait your turn," telling me that I should try for a less prominent role on the city council or school board. My boys like CAC, Earl, T. Chavis, and MG all said just the opposite. Indeed, they all said some version of the same thing to me: "You're overdue. It's been time to step up and lead your community."

Ultimately, I followed my heart and my teachings. I remembered a scripture from Isaiah 6:8. "And I heard the voice of the Lord saying, 'Whom shall I send, and who will go for us?'"

I decided to raise my hand. *Here I am, send me.*

I couldn't sit out. Not this one. It was 2012 and President Obama was running for reelection. As important, a critical backlash against President Obama and the multiracial, progressive politics he represented was taking hold across the nation. To that end, more than a dozen states had passed or were in the process of passing voter suppression laws that would devastate the vote and turn the clock back on voting rights: more strenuous voter ID laws, eliminating same-day registration, impeding voter registration altogether.

The probate judge is the chief election official and the highest administrative officer in the county. Flipping this seat was critical to protecting all voters from the coming backlash. Voting rights was my father's life's work: I couldn't stand by and watch his legacy dismantled.

It was also impossible to ignore the personal digs against me and my father. They hurt. But they forced me to get clear with myself and by extension the voters about who *I* was and what *I* was about. That meant excavating some old insecurities and putting them to bed, once and for all.

I knew I had gone to school out of state and worked jobs out of state, in part to prove to myself and the world that I was my own man. I also knew that my dad and I did not necessarily care about the same issues—at least, not with the same intensity. He was a civil rights man, through and through. I also cared about civil

rights in our community. Deeply. Obviously. But my life experience compelled me to think critically about other issues, too. Who
was looking out for the small business owner? And who was working with those small business leaders to create and cultivate the
workforce of the future? Most importantly, our schools had de-
clined precipitously since the 1970s, when I was in public schools.
Who was willing to go "all in" for kids? Our future?

With President Obama at the top of the ticket—the ultimate
embodiment of a new generation in political leadership—we ran
an inspired race. We cultivated our grassroots leaders and
neighborhood-level community organizers. Most of all, I emphasized motivating unlikely voters and getting them to turn out on
Election Day. If we were going to show—not just tell—Montgomery
that our campaign *wasn't* about the usual suspects (my dad, the
incumbent, the so-called establishment), then we needed to inspire new participation in the process.

Win, lose, or draw, *that* was most important.

Indeed, the moment on the campaign when I thought, *We're
going to win this thing!* was when a young man drove up in a cus-
tom car with twenty-four-inch rims, tinted windows, and music
blaring. We all stopped in our tracks. He rolled down the window,
his aviators reflecting the bright sun, and said plainly, "Steven
Reed, I came out to vote for you, cuz."

That story always moves me when I think about it, because
that's what politics is about. All of us, no matter who we are, matter, and each of us should believe that we matter in our democratic
process because we do. You do.

I won the race for probate judge and became the first Black
person to hold the position. I am proud of that. Most of the work is
uncontroversial but important. The probate judge plays a huge
role in making government work for ordinary people. And to that
end, the biggest improvement we needed to make right away was

in the efficiency and the quality of service throughout the office. Unlocking the potential of entrepreneurs like Miss Sophia was my North Star.

A few years into my tenure, I encountered and confronted a fierce opponent of my ideals of justice in Roy Moore, then the chief justice of the Supreme Court of Alabama. Years later, Moore would go on to run for the United States Senate before losing to Doug Jones in one of the closest elections in history. Allegations of gross sexual misconduct against Moore—and an inspired race by Jones—kept Moore, a disgrace, from that dignified seat.

Roy Moore was proof that Mr. Segregation didn't really die. Indeed, with the help of his son, Mr. Discrimination, Mr. Segregation lived on in new and creative ways while always operating with the goal of dividing us.

Take our schools, for instance. While public schools are desegregated in the eyes of the law, those committed to keeping the races separate, especially within the spheres that count most, like education, engineered workarounds. In 2004, Roy Moore jumped to defend language in Alabama's archaic constitution that mandated "separate schools for white and colored children." Even though *Brown v. Board of Education* had a thing or two to say about it, politicians like Moore were advancing segregation among our kids in both symbolic and substantive ways.

And it's working. In the Alabama Black Belt, where my mother grew up, most Black students in public schools aren't just segregated; they're *isolated*. As white families fled the public schools, they took their tax dollars and investment with them. It triggers a cycle. Those schools struggle before they're designated as "failing," which encourages more families of means, white *and* Black, to leave.

Meanwhile, policy makers resist efforts to create magnet schools or to bus in students from across state-drawn boundaries to prevent integration from happening. The net result is isolated communities that struggle to ever greater degrees. Integration isn't just a moral good. It has practical effects: integrated education increases the likelihood of people of all races getting along and working together. It reduces societal tension and ultimately strengthens the health of our democracy. Students, especially those from less affluent, less privileged backgrounds, demonstrate, on average, better learning gains.

Without integration, we condemn large portions of our state to less healthy and successful lives. Nearly half of the state's "failing" schools—defined as the bottom 6 percent of all schools—are in the Black Belt. It hurts my heart because that's where my family and my ancestors are from. Those who came before us would shed so many tears if they witnessed the state of education in many parts of Alabama. They didn't fight and sacrifice to end up *here*.

What's worse is that, contrary to what many on the right would want you to believe, it's actually white supremacists who practice critical race theory in our schools. Across Alabama and the South, local school boards fight like hell to "whitewash" American history, from presenting the Civil War as a fight to advance the noble cause of states' rights instead of a war over slavery to marginalizing the contributions of the Moses Generation and rewriting the recent history of segregation in America.

In 2015, those discriminatory forces, led by then Chief Justice Moore, returned to where the battle for freedom and equality in the South started: the courthouse. Matters quickly came to a head when the Supreme Court decided in *Obergefell v. Hodges* that love is love and marriage equality is the law of the land.

Being a judge means understanding that when the Supreme Court rules on something, whether you like it or not, it's the law of the land. That's it. They're the final word.

Or at least they should be. But, again, this is Alabama. And this is Montgomery, where even after the U.S. Supreme Court ruled for desegregation in *Brown v. Board of Education*, there was massive, coordinated, racist opposition to fully integrating our schools *for more than a decade*. During that time, the state passed laws and devised regulations with the sole purpose of evading the law of the land as settled by America's highest court.

Using the law to foment lawlessness—only in Alabama.

Looking back on the Moses Generation, we saw the same behavior in the wake of *Browder v. Gayle*, which settled the issue of the bus boycott. Even though the federal government had spoken, there was still pushback against integrating and resistance to following federal orders. The refrain in Alabama since before the Civil War is that "the federal government is telling us what to do, and we won't abide it." This refrain is one of the roots of slavery and, ultimately, the founding of the Confederacy, which uplifted the supremacy of states' rights. Alabama officials resisted federal authority even though the state couldn't fund its schools or hospitals *without* regular federal resources. In a word: hypocrisy. Alabama wanted it both ways: the investment of federal government without upholding the rights it enumerates and calls states to protect.

As probate judge, my perspective on the *Obergefell* decision was simple: if it's a Supreme Court decision, we've got to abide by it. That's just what it is.

However, right after the decision came down, my closest political adviser, Chip Hill, walked into my chambers to inform me that the chief justice of the Alabama Supreme Court just said probate judges didn't have to abide by a U.S. Supreme Court decision. To which I responded, "What the hell do you mean we don't have to abide by it?"

Now, I'm not a lawyer, right? But even I know that when it's a Supreme Court decision, we sure do have to abide by it.

With Chip, I was matter-of-fact. "No, we're going to fight this. We're going to push back against Chief Justice Moore."

I *might* have used more choice language in that conversation. I was angry. Who was the judge to deny good people a chance at marriage when it's the settled law of the land? The chief justice's position was mean-spirited, unkind, and discriminatory to its core. It also hearkened back to the laws against interracial marriage, which governed the country until the 1960s—practically in the span of my own lifetime.

In *Loving v. Virginia*, Mildred and Richard Loving appealed the Virginia state law that invalidated their marriage and threatened to send them both to prison. Over the span of almost ten years, the Lovings petitioned their case first to the Virginia Supreme Court, where the law was upheld, and then to the U.S. Supreme Court, which unanimously struck down Virginia's so-called Racial Integrity Act of 1924 along with all other laws banning or restricting interracial marriage nationwide.

Forty years later, Mildred Loving released this statement on the anniversary of the historic decision:

> My generation was bitterly divided over something that should have been so clear and right. The majority believed that what the judge said, that it was God's plan to keep people apart, and that government should discriminate against people in love. But I have lived long enough now to see big changes. The older generation's fears and prejudices have given way, and today's young people realize that if someone loves someone, they have a right to marry.
>
> Surrounded as I am now by wonderful children and grandchildren, not a day goes by that I don't think of Richard and our love, our right to marry, and how much it meant to me to have that freedom to marry the person precious to me, even if

others thought he was the "wrong kind of person" for me to marry. I believe all Americans, no matter their race, no matter their sex, no matter their sexual orientation, should have that same freedom to marry. Government has no business impos- ing some people's religious beliefs over others. Especially if it denies people's civil rights.

I am still not a political person, but I am proud that Rich- ard's and my name is on a court case that can help reinforce the love, the commitment, the fairness, and the family that so many people, black or white, young or old, gay or straight seek in life. I support the freedom to marry for all. That's what Lov- ing, and loving, are all about.

I was raised by Mildred and Richard's generation. And of their many battles and hard-earned victories, the right to marry, regard- less of one's race, has had one of the biggest impacts on our society. Indeed, President Obama was the by-product of an interracial mar- riage. Many folks across the South remembered when courts re- fused to issue marriage licenses to interracial couples well into the 1970s. That decision by the courts had a powerful shaping effect on the local culture and throughout communities. And even though interracial marriage is the settled law of the land today, many peo- ple still refuse to embrace or acknowledge it. The Supreme Court decision offered Chief Justice Moore a chance to dredge up racist garbage and throw red meat to his base as well as pick on the LGBTQ members of our community—easy targets in Alabama.

Shortly after Chip and I determined our best course forward, I joined a conference call that included every probate judge in the state of Alabama. All sixty-seven counties were represented. Os- tensibly, the call was about the next steps in issuing licenses after the Supreme Court's recent decision. But the call quickly devolved into a debate about whether to issue licenses at all.

I was in no mood to debate. This was ridiculous. I cut right to the chase.

"Of course we're going to issue marriage licenses. It's the Supreme Court that's ruled in this case. How are any of you not going to issue marriage licenses? I thought we had an oath to uphold."

Another probate judge chimed in, "Well, the chief justice is saying he's going to remove us from the bench if we do that."

I called his bluff. "Well, hold on one second. The chief justice doesn't have that authority. Let's go back to Alabama's constitution. It might be archaic. That constitution might even be racist. But nowhere in that document does it say that the chief justice can remove any of us, for any cause, let alone obeying a ruling by the Supreme Court."

The call went around in circles. It wasn't even really a discussion. Despite the fact that nearly seventy probate judges were on the call, and most were lawyers by training and respected jurists, most everyone took turns speaking about their religious beliefs or their cultural upbringing—ultimately, their personal sense of right and wrong on the matter—instead of what the law called for.

On one level, I get it. I grew up with a code—a set of expectations about how to behave, what's moral, what's right. My code is as strong as anyone's.

But this wasn't about our personal conceptions of what's "right"; this was about law. And the law was clear. Love is love. Issue the damn license.

Finally, I cut off one of the probate judges. "Well, your cultural beliefs do not apply to the law. We take an oath to uphold the Constitution of the United States. That's what's at stake here. This isn't about your personal beliefs, whatever they may be."

There was silence. A judge raised his voice. "Well, we're not going to issue any marriage licenses."

I was angry now. "Well, this is going back to what people did in segregation. People always talk about what they would and, more importantly, wouldn't have done in the 1950s and 1960s—but this is no different. This is discrimination, plain and simple."

Another judge chimed in. "Well, we know it's right, but I can't do it because of the political risk. It depends on how my community feels about it."

I had had enough. "Look, I'm going to issue marriage licenses. I know enough about what's right and wrong to do the right thing here. All of you will have to decide which side of history you want to be on, whatever article of faith you're trying to hold on to, or whatever thoughts you might have regarding your interpretation."

Out of sixty-seven judges, only four of us decided to follow the law.

I was joined by the judges in Jefferson County, which is home to the city of Birmingham, and the judge in Chilton County. The four of us agreed that the very next day we would begin to issue licenses.

It wasn't long before the chief justice said that he would send state troopers down to my chambers to remove me from the bench.

It was getting tense now. Black people and law enforcement have a long, painful history. The chief justice knew what he was doing. It was a threat, a dog whistle.

I huddled with my legal team. They confirmed that the chief justice did not have the jurisdiction or power to issue such an order. It didn't mean it *wouldn't* happen, but we were in uncharted waters. I stood firm: I let the chief justice know that "I don't report to the State Supreme Court; I report to the citizens of Montgomery County, who elected me for six years."

As we prepared to issue licenses, we also prepared for the worst. If state troopers *did* arrive in my chambers, we needed a plan. I called our recently elected sheriff, who just happened to be a fraternity brother, Derrick Cunningham.

"Sheriff," I said, "we might have a little drama down here."

"Oh, you're talking about Roy Moore. I wish he would bring his ass down here," Sheriff Cunningham responded. "He would get his ass messed up." Only he didn't say "mess."

Spoken like a true sheriff. Just straight talk.

"Well, look, I appreciate that, Sheriff, but if he tries to have me removed, I want to make sure you got my back."

"Man, I got your back and front," the sheriff said. "You ain't got to worry about that." He added, "I wish he would come in. Listen, I count. You and I count. He'd better realize that."

"Well, there it is," I said before hanging up the phone.

We started issuing licenses. I also took to the news, the radio, the internet, whatever communications medium would have me. Not only were we going to do what was right, but we would make a statement about Montgomery and a statement about Alabama: this wasn't the old Alabama, at least not in the cities. While the vestiges of Mr. Discrimination still exist, there were enough of us in powerful elected positions that could push back on that.

Others stood up as well. Alan King, the probate judge in Jefferson County, played a huge role in that battle. He was a Democrat, white, and a member of the United Methodist Church. He pointed to his faith as a rebuttal to those who were using the church as a rationale for not doing the right thing. He was a second-generation judge who had graduated from the University of Alabama. He had all the bona fides of an Alabama elected official and all the qualifications to stand strong. He made sophisticated legal arguments to substantiate our position. He said over and over, "It's about decisions. It's about doing what's right. It's about following the law."

The evening of the first day we issued licenses, I reflected in my chamber. I thought about the fights of the Moses Generation and the many contributions and sacrifices of those who came before. I was physically tired, but my soul rejoiced from a righteous battle well fought.

I also thought about Lawrence Alfred, the phenomenal recruiter who brought both me and Joey to Morehouse all those years ago.

I thought about the fact that Lawrence was gay. He died a few years ago of AIDS. I thought about the shame and stigma he lived with throughout his life and the fact that even though we loved our institutions, like Morehouse, and our communities, like Montgomery, he could never fully be himself. In his entire life, he never experienced perfect acceptance.

We weren't there yet. We hadn't achieved a society in which everyone was fully accepted. But that night I was glad we took one step closer.

Chapter 8

THE OTHER SIDE
OF THE BALL

Years ago, I played Division II football at Morehouse. After a lot of hard work and sacrifice, I ultimately lettered as a defensive back.

To be successful as a defensive back, you must react, as quickly as you can, to what the offense is doing. Sometimes the quarterback calls an audible and you must shift your position on the field in response; other times he has an option and then you have to prepare for the run or a pass by dropping into zone. Whatever it is, you must read what's unfolding in front of you and be ready to strike when the moment is right.

Well, being a judge is a lot like being a defensive back. Your job is to react to what is brought before you.

In politics, one of the biggest *offensive* players is the executive. Nationally, it's the president. At the state level, it's the governor. Locally, especially in cities, it's the mayor. The executive, through their direct action and leadership, does the most to impact our everyday lives. They govern the systems that keep us safe, educate our children, heal our sick, and provide for those who cannot provide for themselves. The executive makes a thousand decisions every single day that determine our society's success across each of those areas.

And while I loved playing defense in college, the truth is I started on the offensive side of the ball. On offense, I loved how we could control the tempo and pace of the game. With a good plan, we could make things happen, sometimes explosively. But in sports, I wasn't quite built for offense. As I got older, as a smaller guy, I was moved to the defensive side of the ball, where my size was an advantage. It was the right call. I played more and therefore contributed to our team's overall success. It was, given my talents, where I fit best.

Politics was proving to be a different matter altogether. Choosing to issue licenses after the marriage equality decision was important, but in the end I was still *reacting* to events, not shaping them. After a few years in public life, I was growing impatient. Working as a probate judge was effectively working by committee and proved frustrating when I wanted to effect bigger and broader change. Judges across the state and at all levels of the judicial system work—sometimes together, sometimes not—to administer the law. As the marriage equality decision showed, the path to change is often long, winding, and frustrating as we wait on other elements of the system to do the right thing.

I was ready to be the thermostat, not the thermometer.

I first expressed my frustration to my father. My logic was simple: politically speaking, I was comfortable. My seat was "safe." I was already on my way to an easy reelection. If longevity in public service was my goal, all I had to do was put one foot in front of the other and longevity was what I would get. But I wasn't interested in longevity. I wanted results.

Everywhere I looked, we had big problems to solve.

Our schools were in crisis. They badly needed more funding. *Brown v. Board of Education* and a hundred other legal decisions proved that there were limits to what judges could do to invest in children. Without bold political action by a leader who could create consensus among the public to do hard things, like raise taxes, nothing significant would change.

Economically, we were still stuck. As probate judge, I made meaningful and important changes to the way the city ran, especially for Black business owners. I made sure entrepreneurs like Sophia Jackson got their permits. I helped remove government as an obstacle. No doubt, that was important work. But it would take years for that to change the city's economic trajectory. Meanwhile, nearby Huntsville and Birmingham were experiencing explosive growth as they both developed new industries and exploited their

natural advantages in the global economy. They were led by focused leaders who were hungry for their cities to thrive.

I was convinced that Montgomery could follow a similar trajectory, but if the old boys ran the show, we would move too slowly,
invest too little, and only pick winners who looked like the familiar
crowd. We would double down on the formula for stagnation.

To bring Montgomery into the twenty-first century, we needed
to invest in *all* of our city.

Tamika heard my ideas and encouraged me. "You're not one to
sit back and watch the crowd, Steve. Let's face it: you were either
going to do probate judge for a little bit—at least long enough to
change a few big things down there before going back to the private sector—or you were going to end up impatient, as you always
do, and try to do more. It's just who you are."

Tamika knew me as well as anyone. From the moment we first
met, I was in a hurry. Back then, I was in a rush to plan a party. But
since then, I've been in a rush to start a business, to change the
business climate, and then, once I made up my mind to run for
office to shift the political climate. A run for the top job in Montgomery was the biggest, most daunting task yet.

My dad sensed it first. He was supportive, too, but he also cautioned me. "Probate judge is one thing, Steve, and you can do a lot
of good there, and you have. But don't forget: the old boys run the
city. They ain't going to give up all that power without a fight. I
would know. I've spent my career tangling with them."

He was right. And I wasn't scared of the fight per se. But I
wasn't interested in losing. The key question, then, was this: Is
Montgomery ready for a change? A *big* change? Winning would require a broad coalition of voters, Black and white, to upset the
setup at City Hall. Montgomery, as an electorate, didn't like change.
My theory was that the residents had lived through too much of it

from the civil rights years. The city's underlying conservatism was reflected in its elected leadership. Since the 1970s we had installed only a handful of leaders in the top job. Those individuals ruled for decades while the city stagnated.

I also took offense at the racial undertones of those critiques or cautions. In all my life, I've never, ever heard someone say that a *white* person has too much power. Never. Yet, when Black leaders commit to serve and are trusted by the public with power, it isn't long before the grumbling starts. But that doesn't change one core fact: representation matters because *empathy*, and *lived experience*, matter in the practice of leadership.

And the truth of the matter is that Montgomery was struggling to adapt and to keep up with the times. And while we were struggling, the community was hurting; that much was clear. And leadership—which doesn't turn over that much—didn't get it. The last three mayors had held the job for at least a decade each; one served for twenty-two years. But those leaders prized longevity over performance. As I moved from conversation to conversation with pastors and parents, in living rooms and church sitting rooms, I heard the same thing, over and over: "We're tired. We want more for, and demand more from, Montgomery and Alabama."

What struck me was that white and Black residents *alike* shared that same frustration and expressed a similar sentiment. Even the long-standing racial divisions were falling away. People, all people, just wanted better.

Montgomery was getting left behind in this century because we couldn't get out of the last century.

Whether it was a new police chief, better-funded schools, or a belief that we could do better—so much better—all roads led to one role and one role only: mayor. I was ready to serve and I felt called to serve. I was frustrated, too, and believed I had the skills, perspective, and experience to guide the city forward.

I declared my candidacy. I opened the campaign with a simple statement: "It's time for Montgomery to not only survive but thrive."

The campaign for mayor was crowded and intense. Out of a dozen candidates, six of them were "front-runners" at various points in the race, and ten of them were Black. That last fact was notable because Montgomery had never elected a Black mayor. The winds of change were blowing.

The race was competitive, but I went back to what I knew from my days as an entrepreneur: Control the controllables and execute our plan.

And our plan for this race was to build a movement. I didn't just want to win; I wanted a mandate. And only the people could deliver that by overwhelmingly electing a leader. That would require bridging ancient divides between Black and white voters, young and old, those who lived downtown and those on the city's outskirts.

For some reason I could sense from the very beginning of the race that the city was ready. I had spent much of my life in Montgomery, and for the first time in my life the people of the city were unified in their dissatisfaction and were calling for the same thing: progress for everyone. Enough of the old battles and enough losing the fights of our lives: we wanted a chance to compete in the world economy; schools capable of delivering a good life for every person, no matter their color; a true, abiding sense of safety and security.

The only scary moment in the election, for me, was the entry of the Elvis impersonator. Never underestimate the King.

In all seriousness, the race culminated in a runoff between me and David Woods, which represented a fork-in-the-road moment for Montgomery. David was a local media mogul who owned three television stations, including an affiliate of Fox News. There were many differences between us, but the biggest was our willingness to *invest* in our city. Fundamentally, we needed to deploy more resources to secure our safety, our children, our communities, but David had a hard line against any measures that would raise revenue. I believed we had cut Montgomery down to the bone, so much so that the city was barely hanging on to a chance at a brighter future.

We needed to stop talking out of both sides of our mouths.

We couldn't say that we needed more and better police officers—capable of taking the time to do real community policing—without investment.

We couldn't say that we needed schools with more and better teachers—capable of helping every child learn no matter their circumstance—without investment.

We couldn't say that we needed to see development in Montgomery's many disinvested neighborhoods, to drive up property values and invite residents back into the city, without investment.

We won't cut our way to success. We've tried that.

It was time to unify and invest in a slate of priorities capable of propelling us forward, together.

In the end, we won, and won overwhelmingly: 67 percent of Montgomery voters came together to deliver me to City Hall. The number I am most proud of from the campaign? Our race saw a 25 percent increase in voter turnout—with many voting for the very first time. Just like my race for probate judge, our most important goal was reaching every single voter. We knocked on thousands of doors and deployed organizers to every neighborhood in the city. We left no stone unturned; I wanted every resident to hear from us.

The mayoral race had a different feel from my race for probate judge. In 2012, I was the underdog. There were many people—in the Black and white communities—who doubted my ability to win and said so. For the mayoral race, from the start, we knew—everyone knew—that we were the favorite to win, with one big caveat: there's winning and then there's winning with a mandate. Without a mandate we couldn't change anything. With a mandate, we would live up to the promise that comes with ushering in a new generation of leadership.

In that, there's a lesson. Winning the mayor's seat wasn't about a title or the prestige of the position. It was about making life better for the residents of Montgomery and doing the hard thing—for our children, for our communities, for our business owners, *for our future*. That meant taking on a set of entrenched interests that would be extremely difficult to defeat with a community coming together to say, "Enough."

At our victory party, I said, "This election has never been about me. It has never been about my ideas. It has been about the hopes and dreams we have as individuals and collectively in this city. The beauty of what we've been able to do, from Newtown to Downtown, is that this city can improve outcomes for everyone regardless of their neighborhood, their zip code, or anything that may divide us or make us different from one another. We've been focused from day one on the things that make us better, the things that unite us. This is what I see in the results of tonight: a unified Montgomery."

My inner circle had been there during the campaign. Friends flew in and drove from all over the country to help us campaign. They even brought their kids, which made it fun, but also made us feel old. My election was now a culminating moment in our lives.

We didn't celebrate long. The transition started immediately. We needed to build a team and assemble the best people, who had to be ready to hit the ground running on day one of my administration. I also set my sights on a huge goal that I was determined to accomplish above all else: increasing school funding. That would require a referendum and another vote.

Inauguration day was special. My dad spoke and dispensed wisdom. He made it clear that "I know I'm not the mayor, don't want to be, ain't trying to be," which made me chuckle. If my dad were my age, he'd probably be the mayor—a good one, too—for a long time.

My mother smiled. And smiled. And smiled. I don't think I've ever seen her so happy or proud.

We had to change venues because so many folks came from all over. Morehouse men were deep. My frat, Omega Psi Phi Fraternity, Inc., was deep. Twenty-two other mayors from across the country came in for the occasion. The election was covered nationally and internationally.

When I gave my address, I wanted to step back from the community that raised me, to appreciate the election for the milestone it was before charting a big, bold plan. We needed to do both.

Today, we are assembled here because we chose destiny over division. Today, we are assembled here because we chose the future over fear. Therefore, because of our hearts and our actions, I stand here in a position that many of those who were sold on the banks of the Alabama River, just a few feet from here, could only have imagined. This is a culmination of those distant dreams.

Loyalty, faith, and perseverance are the pillars that have built this community. Let us mark this day in remembrance of who we are and how far we've come. We have a duty to ourselves in this society. This is the meaning of living our creed. This is why the son whose parents were not even served in a local restaurant just up the street, and whose father led sit-in protests for equal treatment under the law, can now take this oath and help write laws that apply equally to all.

Chapter 9

THE PROBLEMS THAT ARE OPPORTUNITIES

I first heard the word *COVID* in late January 2020.

I was at the U.S. Conference of Mayors. I had just taken office. And it was an exciting time. The conference offered a singular opportunity to connect with peers around the country who were also leading cities. As a new mayor and the first Black person in the role in Montgomery, it was also a powerful opportunity to find and build community.

One note on that: You must identify rituals and relationships to help you restore yourself. All my life I've committed to regular exercise (these days, a light jog to start my day) and a stable of relationships to help with the isolation and pressure that follows intense leadership experiences. I always advise leaders who are up and coming to invest in a tight-knit group of peers who truly understand what they're going through as they do the work. It's even better if these individuals relate to you in direct and personal ways. I am a better mayor, and a better man, because I have other leaders in my life. I am, for instance, on a text thread with other Black mayors who are grappling with similar issues. As mayors of large and complex cities, they understand the challenge in front of me. As Black men, they can relate to the unique burdens that come with the job. I am also regularly in touch with a group of elder statesmen who were in similar roles a few decades ago. They remind me that there's nothing ever truly new about our challenges and to stay on the righteous course. They bring perspective. If you're serious about sustaining yourself in the work—doing the marathon that is life—building your tribe is hugely important.

In fact, I've seen a lot of talented, supersmart leaders who *didn't* have a practice for personal restoration lose their way. Stress, and the relentless pressure that almost always follows big jobs in public service, can drive a person crazy. Finding ways to manage that stress is essential to keeping "the crazy" at arm's length. Remember: burnout, losing your way, getting lost in the job—it can happen to anyone.

For all these reasons and more, I was excited to be at the U.S. Conference of Mayors. I was anxious to build the relationships and personal connections I knew would support me in my new role and, more critically, position Montgomery for transformative investment.

I was surprised, then, when my old friend Dewardric McNeal, whom we call DL, kept calling my cell. I screened his call initially; I'd get back to him when I was home and catching up on correspondence.

But the phone kept ringing.

Maybe this was important. When he called back, I picked up.

"What's up, DL? You good?" I asked right away. I was warm and glad to speak with him, but there was a hint of impatience in my voice.

"Hey, Steve, yeah, I am good, and I am sorry to bother you like this, but I thought you'd want to know, given everything that's happening with your new job."

"Yeah, what's that?"

"Keep an eye on COVID," DL started, his tone urgent and insistent. "Watch what's happening in China. It's not clear exactly *when* it's coming here, but it's a virtual certainty. We're about to encounter a once-in-a-generation crisis."

To be fair, I had *not* been watching what was happening in China up until that point. Admittedly, my concerns were closer to home. I was about to rediscover, for the first time since my days at American Airlines, just how interconnected our world truly is.

"What the hell is COVID?" I asked, confused.

"It's a virus, Steve. A flu—but way worse. And it's spreading like wildfire in China, and it's coming to America—hell, it's already here on the coasts—but it'll hit every corner of this country before it's over with. You don't need me to tell you that Montgomery is a major hub, man, and the virus could already be in your city somewhere."

DL was a China expert. He knew that country and its geopolitics as well as anyone. *This* was why he was blowing up my phone.

"Well, what do we do about it?" I asked as my mind turned on the possibilities.

"Just get ready, Steve. Be ready."

"Okay, man, I'll investigate it. I appreciate the call."

Immediately after hanging up, I dialed my chief of staff. "Chip, track down everything you can on COVID—C-O-V-I-D. Apparently a tidal wave is coming. We better get ready."

Chip moved quickly, and back in Montgomery he worked with Mike Bloomberg's team to set up a call, for when I was back, with the top infectious disease experts in the United States. Zeke Emanuel, brother of former Obama chief of staff Rahm Emanuel and a top expert in public health, closed with sobering words:

"The pandemic isn't going to last weeks. I am sorry. You shouldn't count in *days*. This will stretch on for months. The only question is how many."

I put the call on mute and turned to Chip.

"Seriously???" I mouthed to him. His eyes bulged in response.

✳ ✳ ✳

Just sixty days later, I stood at a podium in a cold, dimly lit city auditorium. "The stakes are basically life-and-death," I started. Before me was a kind of dystopia. The press corps was spread out, socially distanced. They stood before me, rigid and masked, their eyes squinting in concern. The mood was entirely dreary. "I don't know how to put it more starkly than that," I continued. "We're looking at potentially hundreds of thousands of Americans dying because of this virus. We're looking at potentially thousands of Alabamians dying because of this virus."

Since I first learned about COVID-19 from DL, it was only a matter of time before the virus spread throughout Alabama. From early February 2020, we worked around the clock to prepare Montgomery for the pandemic. The biggest challenge up front? Convincing a skeptical public to shelter in place, at least until our medical system got a handle on the first wave, and to take the necessary behavioral precautions through the life of the pandemic: social distancing, masking, and quarantining when exhibiting symptoms.

To say that my first year in office got off to a fast start is an understatement. Just months after my inauguration, we were battling a once-in-a-century public health crisis in the age of disinformation and in the Deep South. While I had just won the confidence of the public in a historic election, all of my goodwill was instantly put to the test. I'll be blunt: no political leader wants to dictate terms of any sort to their fellow Americans, who are independent by nature, especially in the South. And doubly so in Alabama. And yet, that's where I found myself in March of 2020.

"We have say-so in what happens: we can increase or decrease the number who die by our behavior," I continued at the press conference. I leveled with the public. "What does this community choose to do? Do we take this seriously? Are we willing to police our friends, our neighbors, our church members? That could mean a polite nudge or an encouraging word. But some of the things that have been going on can no longer take place. We have to take the necessary precautions."

As the virus spread, we worked with Maxwell Air Force Base and every organ of city government to put Montgomery on an emergency footing: we canceled public events, shut down public facilities, and diverted all available medical personnel to triage care. We stockpiled supplies and messaged relentlessly through public television, radio, social media, and the internet.

I enlisted other trusted voices, including Dr. David Thrasher, a brilliant clinician who knew how to relate to the average Alabamian. He was Montgomery's Dr. Fauci, and he joined me at several early press conferences.

"Well," David started in his deep Southern drawl, "we're behind New York [in our COVID-19 incidence rate]. We're behind them probably by two or three weeks. That's why I say the next thirty days are going to be hell for America and hell for Alabama.

"I'll give you an example," he continued. "Take a fishpond. Everybody here knows what a fishpond is. Put one lily pad in that fishpond. If it doubles every day, it won't cover the entire pond until day sixty. On day fifty-nine, only half of the pond is covered. On fifty-four it's only 20 percent. We're at 20 percent. It's going to go straight up. This pond will be full of death and patients if we don't do what Mayor Reed is telling us."

Dr. Thrasher really knew how to lay it on you.

I wasn't fazed. I felt everything in my life had prepared me for this moment—a critical opportunity to lead. But I was concerned, and without a doubt I went into the job every day more focused than I had ever been in any job at any moment in my entire life.

Ever since the call with Zeke Emanuel, I leaned into one central truth as we navigated COVID: this is our moment of crisis. In my mind, I went back to my training. In school, particularly if you've been as fortunate as I have been to study business and leadership at a top school like Vanderbilt, you study crisis. You learn from the models—the greats—across the private and public sectors. You read about Lee Iacocca and what he did to turn Chrysler around. Obviously, you study the turnaround miracle that was Apple under Steve Jobs. You spend time with leaders like the late, great Reginald F. Lewis, Ken Chenault of American Express, and Ursula Burns of Xerox, who disrupted incumbent industries. You study the legends—entrepreneurs like A. G. Gaston, one of Alabama's finest business leaders.

Across the study of crisis management, the response is always different. The one thing all those leaders had in common, however, was that *they never wasted a crisis.* A crisis wasn't just a problem to solve. Great leaders do not focus only on the acute problem in front of them—the supposed root of the crisis; rather, they look ahead to the future and consider the possibilities. They ask themselves, *How do we shift this problem to a moment of transformation? As we're tested, how do we cultivate a new spirit in our people and emerge stronger?*

Apple didn't just beat bankruptcy; it emerged as the most innovative company in the world. Churchill didn't just weather Hitler's bombings; he forged a grand Western alliance that serves as the bulwark for democracy to this day.

In Montgomery, we needed to think bigger than the problem before us. What did the crisis mean for our city's transformation? How could we ensure that our people would emerge from this chapter stronger?

☀ ☀ ☀

As COVID raged on, it was clear that the pandemic was making the future come faster. Before COVID, just a handful of professionals worked from home. During COVID and beyond, the incidence of remote work exploded. For a city like Montgomery, there's opportunity in that. We could, if we're smart, position our city to capture a larger share of the professional workforce suddenly up for grabs.

COVID changed the way our children learn and what they needed to learn. If STEM education was important before, it's essential in an economy that relies almost exclusively on technology and software to run.

Coming into office, my single biggest priority was to address the long and consequential neglect of our public schools. COVID raised the stakes. Our children needed an unprecedented level of investment to come out of the pandemic in better shape than when we entered this mess, and if our city was going to compete and emerge as one of the great winners in the twenty-first century, we needed to produce a workforce that could navigate the new environment.

We had work to do. In my lifetime, Montgomery public schools saw their enrollment and investment per pupil decline precipitously year over year. By the 1990s the city of Montgomery was investing the bare minimum in the public schools, ranking near or at the bottom, nationally.

The consequences were severe. Too many students, especially Black students, were condemned to futures that were less bright and less healthy because we did not live up to our obligation to invest in their success.

I also knew that, politically, tackling this challenge was dangerous. After all, in the 1990s, my father was part of the failed campaign to pass a referendum that would increase taxes for the schools. This was politically complicated territory that had burned other leaders in the past.

But I didn't run for mayor to worry about longevity in office. And I wasn't about to waste a crisis. We were doing big things to respond to COVID, and I was challenging Montgomery's tired political culture to think differently and act bigger, bolder, and more decisively. I wasn't going to lower our aims now.

Besides, this was personal.

I am a proud graduate of our public schools. I've seen them work. They set me on my life's trajectory. My life is a testament to their power. I wasn't just raised by an extraordinary set of parents; I was raised by a village that started at school.

That's not to say my schooling was perfect. It wasn't. There were curriculum choices that were wrongheaded and some teachers with other agendas. But, overall, I couldn't have asked for a better start in life.

Every student—no matter their race—deserves that start.

Going back to my campaign for mayor, I *knew* I would take this on in the first one hundred days. What I didn't know was that we would do so during a once-in-a-generation global pandemic. During the race for mayor, I told my team, "Keep everything in our campaign machine intact, even after we win. We'll be out here again in a year campaigning to save our schools. Stay ready."

And that's exactly what we did. We kept a lot of the team in place, and the infrastructure that supported the race for mayor was repurposed for our schools. I needed to prosecute a hard—some would say impossible—case during a global crisis.

For starters, we were going to raise taxes.

The shock! The horror!

Yep, we needed to raise taxes to create a world-class education system for our children. After all, for decades, Montgomery led the nation in terms of how *little* we invested in our schools and our children. What had that done for us? Absolutely nothing. That might work for Walmart, but it's not how you build a world-class city with a bright future.

I decided our investment was commensurate with our level of expectations for our schools and our children. Both were too low. That had created a culture in which we scapegoated our schools, our teachers, and our children for their poor performance.

Enough was enough.

We needed to stop blaming poor Black kids. We needed to stop blaming underpaid teachers. We needed to stop blaming unsupported parents. We needed to stop pretending the system was *perfect* when it educated a majority *white* student body.

It was time to make a commitment. It was time to invest. It was time to raise our standards.

I thought about my dad and his childhood. I thought about how we had to build our own schools, with our hands, and with our own money. I thought about the fact that, for decades, we didn't "deserve" to be educated but merely *trained*. I thought about the fact that sixty years out from the tragedies of Jim Crow, thousands of Black students in our city still received an education that was no better than the one students received at the height of segregation. And I thought about the fact that our globalized world, and our competitive knowledge economy, was only going to grow *more* difficult for our students in the wake of COVID-19. We risked leaving thousands of our kids behind, likely forever.

I earned a mandate with my election. Our coalition, large and uncomfortable, was assembled. Surely, the grind and shared sacrifice of COVID-19, as well as the realities of governance, would only work like gravity on my approval ratings. It was now or never. And besides, what was it all for if we weren't here to do what was right for our kids and our future?

And so, at the height of the pandemic, I issued a challenge to the residents of Montgomery.

"I am asking you to join me in the most consequential campaign of our lifetimes, and I include my own election in that. Investing in our children is the most important thing we can do."

I started with the facts, which spoke for themselves: Montgomery public schools receive roughly $1,300 a year in local money per pupil. Huntsville receives $4,000. Tuscaloosa gets $3,200; $3,000 in Opelika; $2,700 in Auburn; $2,400 for Birmingham. No matter the comparison, we were spending about half, or even less, of what our peer cities spent. My proposal would increase taxes to double investment in our schools.

I pressed the public hard. "If you want a return, you have to put something into it," I said. "And for decades we have not done that, and it's shown. It's shown not only in education, but it's shown in our anemic economic growth, and it's shown in our small population growth . . . not just in Montgomery but in all of central Alabama."

I connected investment in our schools to our economic competitiveness—the number one issue facing Montgomery. "What I don't think we've comprehended is that we're in a global race for talent and resources. And if we lose a surgeon to Murfreesboro, Tennessee, or we lose a teacher to Kennesaw, Georgia, or we lose an accountant to Allen, Texas, it's hard to say, 'Well, it's cheaper to live here.' Not everyone is looking for the cheapest product. Most people want a quality product. And that includes where they live and what type of things they have.

"Ultimately, cities are trying to do the same thing, and we're in a global competition for jobs and for people who can fill these jobs. To help our residents obtain good jobs by developing them for the economy would make the biggest difference in our future. But if we don't have the resources to do that, then it's going to be a lot harder for us to compete and therefore keep up with other cities in Alabama and across the United States."

Before setting out for the campaign trail, again I sat down with my dad. He was in the fight the *first* time they tried to raise taxes to invest in the schools. He was there when they failed.

I studied the failure. What went wrong and what needed to be different this time to *win* on this issue. I was straight with my dad: "Pops, y'all blew it back in the 1990s," I observed.

He laughed. And nodded in agreement. I waited for his response. It didn't come. Uncharacteristically, he remained silent. He gestured. He was listening. I continued.

"When y'all did it the first time, there were several things that you failed on. For starters, you all only halfway did it; you weren't all in. You didn't put your best foot forward or get your best organizers and campaigners on the referendum. This time we're taking *my campaign*—the strongest political organization in the city today— and putting them to work on this issue as if our lives depend on it.

"Second, political leadership wasn't behind it. Your membership was divided and didn't speak with one voice on this issue. Our opponents easily divided us as we fell into infighting.

"Third, you didn't invest. You threatened to raise taxes but didn't spend any money upfront to educate people about the *investment* they were making in their children, their schools, and their workforce. You didn't describe the new school buildings or highlight the higher salaries or underscore the new childcare options that would come from their tax dollars. Finally, you didn't connect the dots for the voter: if you're renting and struggling to make ends meet, you're *not* paying this tax. But everyone is benefiting."

I paused. And held my breath. I'd laid a lot on him.

"You missed one thing," he said finally.

"What's that?"

"We didn't have *you*."

He had a point. Controlling the bully pulpit of the city's mayoral office was a big deal. I could, on this issue, control the terms of the debate. While money is not a silver bullet for our schools' challenges, I was adamant that in Montgomery it *must* be part of the equation because we've underinvested for so long. Part of the hangover from the 1960s resulted from an unwillingness to invest in the *public*—our schools, our parks, our people, our neighborhoods. It was almost as if a contingent of white residents and elements of the business community conspired to resist any public effort, now that the "public" included Black people.

That contorted calculus ended with my election and my administration. That wrongheaded view was holding us back. Under my predecessors, we didn't just stagnate; we were left behind.

Fortunately, I discovered during the campaign that most of Montgomery's major stakeholders agreed with me.

I enlisted Maxwell Air Force Base, which has been in Montgomery since the 1930s and has 12,000 active-duty, reserve, civilian, and contract employees working there. It's one of our most significant anchor employers.

I asked Brigadier General Trent Edwards to join us at a press conference to spell out the stakes. Edwards contrasted the Air Force's commitment to training and education to Montgomery's. "We do not invest the bare minimum and expect the best results." He also pointed out that more than half of the airmen stationed at Maxwell come without their families because of the poor standing of the school system.

I emphasized that Montgomery risked losing Maxwell if the referendum to increase investment in the schools failed. "We've been given every indication by military leaders, both past and present, that there was a possibility that Maxwell could leave if our community did not improve our schools' standing. They're not threatening us. It's a matter of fact."

I campaigned vigorously for the referendum. That was essential. I was betting my entire mayorship on the imperative that we invest in our children. And our city had a track record of trying to cut its way to success.

I didn't fear failure. I figured we would either succeed and enact generational change for our children or we would fail, and that would be clarifying. Montgomery elected me to make good on bold promises. Putting our children first would be a good litmus test for our ability to make similar investments in our public safety and our economy. If we couldn't succeed here, then the likelihood we would get it right elsewhere was low.

In the end, the referendum passed—decisively, too. Sixty-one percent of residents voted for the tax increase. In a global pandemic. The experts counseled fear. And our city chose courage.

I was so pleased with the result. It was a watershed moment for our city.

After we won the referendum, I reminded our city that we wanted new residents, businesses, and tourists to choose our city not just for its history and what people can learn from it but for our future and the part they can play in it.

Chapter 10

REWRITING THE NARRATIVE

C hange is hard. But why?

Change *isn't* hard because things are necessarily different.

Change *isn't* hard because we can't do or perform the new thing.

Change *is* hard because *people view change through the lens of loss*.

I'll say it again: people view change through the lens of loss.

Change, even if it's good for us, requires that we give something up. Want to lose weight? No more chocolate chip cookies. Want to buy a house? No more eating out; it's time to save up. Want to improve your grades? That probably means fewer nights out with your friends.

Even when change is a good thing, people *hate* to lose things. Even when they must.

Think about it. As much as everyone says they want change or even *demand* change, we usually fight like hell to keep things from changing. And we fight, usually, because we fear what we might lose.

Communities, even cities, aren't very different from people. As a collective, we also fear change. As I write this, I am halfway through my first term as mayor, and I am amazed at the level of resistance we encounter as we pursue even the most incremental changes. But it makes sense: any change makes us confront who we are and what we must shed today to grow into who we want to be tomorrow.

And change is what we must embrace if we're going to write a new narrative in the South. For me, that change begins with Montgomery, the South's historic capital and a harbinger of what's possible in this region of the country.

The truth is, for too long, Montgomery has settled for doing just fine. We've come to accept okay as good enough—with some believing that okay is *great*. But to change and do something different begins with the admission that over all those years we *weren't* good enough. And we *weren't* great. We were only okay. Sometimes we were worse than okay.

That's real. And that's hard.

In Montgomery, my administration is working to change the culture from the inside out. That change begins with measuring our results—how our kids fare in school, how our economy competes, the safety of our neighborhoods—against the best. For too long, we've been comfortable with low standards instead of investing in our community to create better outcomes and accepting the scrutiny and occasionally the disappointment of coming up short after trying for more and better.

We've changed our approach to governance. We shifted the language we use to describe our city and our future. We aren't interested *only* in the past. Our history is important but our future more so. Our city is home to extraordinary growth industries and a culture that nurtures the entrepreneur and small businesses. We are a safe place to live that welcomes people of all backgrounds.

The net result?

People are interested in Montgomery again. We are open for business.

That doesn't mean we run from our history. We have world-class assets in institutions like the Equal Justice Initiative's now legendary museum, which attracts hundreds of thousands of visitors to our city each year. When people come here, they are often overcome with emotion as they chart America's journey from slavery to Reconstruction to Jim Crow to the fall of segregation. And inevitably they trace recent history to the present day: the backlash of the current moment is painfully clear, as is our role to do something about it. As more people and businesses embrace their responsibility to create a better, fairer world, many now consider Montgomery to be part of their story. Businesses and families are starting to relocate here.

As we tell our story and prosecute our case, we're also confronting a long-standing bias against the South held by much of the country. I am always a little amused when people say, "We don't have a racial problem in our community." To which I always respond, "Well, who have you talked to?" Statements like that usually come from people who haven't considered the perspective of those who are a little bit different from them—people who might live and work in the shadows of our community and economy.

The diversity of America is undeniable. Our nation will continue to diversify. To thrive in this century, our nation must finally confront its sickness around race. Whether you live in Minneapolis, Minnesota; Buffalo, New York; or Charleston, South Carolina, you'll encounter tragic examples of race-based violence. Those cities—and countless others—evoke painful memories that are recent and fresh for many of us.

Those tragedies still overwhelm, and yet the violence that created them is nothing new.

Today, in the twenty-first century, we have a unique opportunity to learn from our history and, yes, learn from the South. Our region can and should be America's mirror. If you look hard and long enough, you'll see your true reflection, warts and all.

As Americans, if we let go of the South, we lose a whole lot of soul. Without our soul, our country is not as just and authentic as it should be. As the capital of the South, our task in Montgomery is to live up to the responsibility with which we've been entrusted. My job as mayor is to lead our city in proving to ourselves and the rest of the world that the South is a powerful engine of progress for people and for our nation.

That job is one of relentless responsibility. It's a sacrifice I gladly make. Some roles—some callings—are for a season. This is one of them.

Every meeting, every minute, is a chance to shape the future of the city I love.

It's hard work, but I love it. I love the chance to build a legacy that is founded on the work of my parents' generation, a legacy I can hand down to my children to inspire them to do their part when it's their turn.

Balancing the impulse to give everything to the job without neglecting my ultimate responsibility to my kids, especially my young boys, is a work in progress. I am, to be sure, extremely lucky: Tamika is an extraordinary mother. And even with COVID-19 raging, I try to stay engaged in a routine, which helps me but especially benefits my young boys. My days start early with a workout—a light jog or, if there's time in the schedule, a visit to the gym—followed by breakfast with my kids (a ritual I've continued from my parents) and then a slate of back-to-back meetings at City Hall on topics as wide-ranging as our public health response, our schools, trash pickup, and planning a new dedication in our historic civil rights district. Those operational meetings are punctuated with the performative elements of the job: ribbon cuttings, public appearances, press conferences.

Work runs late most evenings, especially when we have legislation to get through the city council. There's the usual arm-twisting and cajoling, last-minute phone calls and frantic texts. Running a city oscillates between keeping a small group of people on the same page, stepping back to manage a workforce of 2,500, and speaking directly to hundreds of thousands of people when it's time to pull together for a common cause. The job keeps you on your toes.

Some evenings and most weekends I carve out time to watch

my boys compete in sports. They love it. Just like I did. And part of me still lives vicariously through them as they run to the net and kick the soccer ball.

With respect to administration priorities, I was faced with a choice. On the one hand, we could focus solely on managing the COVID-19 pandemic and put our other plans on hold. No one would blame us if we went this route. The pandemic kept everyone in city government working around the clock.

Or we could walk and chew bubble gum at the same time. We could manage the pandemic *and* advance the agenda on which we campaigned, knowing full well that the virus, our response, and the economic toll it exacted would drag my approval rating down over time. This was surely the harder road.

It was an easy call. We had to push ahead and try to fulfill our campaign promises. I trusted our residents and the coalition of voters who elected us. I figured they knew that every city in America, and indeed the world, was responding to the pandemic. While we needed to take that response seriously, we also had a responsibility to do the work we came here to do: our police force needed new direction, our schools demanded investment, and we had an economy to reinvent.

Besides, why waste a crisis?

Beyond our children and our schools, there was the issue of criminal justice.

The racial reckoning of 2020 opened many people's eyes to the struggle for fair and equitable law enforcement in the United States. After George Floyd's death, communities across Montgomery peaceably assembled to process the loss and strategize about how to move forward. Candlelight vigils were held across the city over a span of months to memorialize all those we, as Americans and Alabamians, have lost to police violence, including now household names such as Breonna Taylor and Ahmaud Arbery.

When George Floyd was murdered in late May 2020, Montgomery, like every other major city in America, took to the streets in protest.

Mr. Floyd died on May 25 after Minneapolis police officer Derek Chauvin pressed his knee on Mr. Floyd's neck for more than eight minutes even after he became unresponsive and had no pulse. The officer was eventually charged with murder and manslaughter. Mr. Floyd's death set off a firestorm across the United States.

Montgomery was no exception. Mr. Floyd's murder had the potential to unleash justified fury after decades of simmering tensions. It was already happening in Alabama. Just up the road, in our sister city, Birmingham, protests devolved into riots and their mayor was forced to implement a city curfew.

I had seen this movie before. An injustice happens. People peaceably assemble—their constitutional right—to express their pain and frustration and to demand change. A relatively small group destroys property and an entire movement is discredited as the state cracks down and disbands the people.

Montgomery has lived through decades of this. We needed to get ahead of it. I went to E. D. Nixon Elementary School to give an address to the community members assembled there. I started my address with empathy.

"I share your outrage over the killing of George Floyd," I began. I voiced my dismay at America continuing to fall short of its founding creed. And I counseled restraint. "We must not further inflict damage upon ourselves, our community, to express our understandable frustration and anger."

I asked the community to consider what they could do to honor the lives lost by helping us change the city for the better, for the long term.

I tied our moment back to E. D. Nixon, a civil rights titan who predated the great Dr. King and Rosa Parks. Mr. Nixon was revered by my elders because he was widely viewed as having taken the first step: he started when the night was still very dark and the dawn many years away. Our community came to realize that in the matter of police reform we had to live up to E. D. Nixon's example by laying a careful and deliberate foundation so that we could deliver critically needed reform. There were decades of vested interests to untangle, and any misstep—including violent riots—would set our cause back for years.

The address worked, and Montgomery stayed peaceful. Despite our pain, we reached for progress.

✳ ✳ ✳

On December 5, 1969, the mayor of Montgomery, Earl James, wrote a letter addressed to the mayor of Montgomery in 2019, two hundred years after the city's founding, when Montgomery's first settlers established the city as a trading port in the transatlantic slave trade along the Alabama River. When Mayor James wrote the letter, I am not sure he would have envisioned that the future mayor reading his note would be Black. Here's what he said:

Dear Mr. Mayor of the city of Montgomery in the year 2019, what a great experience you are having this year, 2019, opening this capsule. I wish I could be around to enjoy the occasion and to see if our dreams of today, 1969, of the things that come to Montgomery have finally taken place. The people of Montgomery are very enthusiastic about the growth of their city. At the present time, we are a city of 163,000 people, representing a New South, and projecting our thoughts to a dynamic future.

We expect to be a city of a quarter of a million people in 1975. Next year, the Alabama River will be developed, whereby barge lines can go from here to the port of Mobile, Alabama, and then to all ports of the world. Our airport, Dannelly Field, has grown

rapidly in the last several years. This growth will continue.
Maxwell Field and Gunter Field, our military bases, play a
predominant part in the economic, cultural, and educational
growth of our community.

This city has always been proud of its public school systems.
And we are very proud that Auburn University is now locating
here, and will open during the year 1971. Montgomery gives a lot
of importance to its young people. It is our desire for our city to
grow for these young people, and upon completing their higher
education, for them to return to their hometown, find
employment, and make their contributions to its welfare. Mr.
Mayor, I hope your problems will be few and your blessings will be
many.

Sincerely, Earl D. James, Mayor

The letter reminded me of something I heard Ken Chenault, former CEO and chairman of American Express, say when I was in graduate school: "It is not the strongest or the most intelligent who survive, but those who are most adapted to change. Over the past ten years, the need for and focus on adaptability has accelerated."

I love Mayor James's letter because he was clear on the results he wanted to see for Montgomery. There's accountability in that for those of us who are alive today and charged with guiding Montgomery into the future. Mayor James envisioned a city that would grow its population, that would be a world leader, and he remarked, with pride, on the quality of our public schools.

It's very important for the mayor of Montgomery to understand where we are as a community and where we want to be. The number one job of a leader is to help your team, and the community you serve, begin with the end in mind. Answer the question: Where do we want to go and how will we get there? The late congressman John Lewis, one of my heroes, said it best:

Take a long, hard look down the road you will have to travel once you have made a commitment to work for change. Know that this transformation will not happen right away. Change often takes time. It rarely happens all at once. In the movement, we didn't know how history would play itself out. When we were getting arrested and waiting in jail or standing in unmovable lines on the courthouse steps, we didn't know what would happen, but we knew it had to happen.[1]

Mayor James had a vision of where to go but didn't know how to get us there—but he knew it had to happen. When I assumed office in 2019, I shared his urgency and felt the responsibility to make it happen. In the decades since Mayor James's tenure, Montgomery simply has not made the progress he envisioned. When we study the facts of Montgomery's performance, we see that we have not done enough to keep up with our global competition. The modest goals Mayor James laid out for 1975, like reaching a population of a quarter million, will not come true until *2045* if the present trends hold.

We must ask ourselves: Where do we want to be? How do we want to get there? And what are we willing to do to make it happen?

For starters, we will have to embrace adaptability—and investigate our willingness to change—to build a future in which Montgomery competes with the best cities in the world.

We can't focus only on the history of social change in Montgomery. We must *change* to realize a brighter future.

The South isn't stuck in the past. Cities in the New South have outgrown us over the last few decades.

What these cities have in common is that they've adapted.

They've changed. They've evolved. They've been willing to take on best practices and do things that were outside the norm for themselves. They understood that diversity was a strength. They understood that it wasn't good enough for power to be held in just a few hands. They understood that they couldn't stay where they were just because it was comfortable. They understood that the challenge really lay in finding ways to compete, not just among themselves, but among those in their region, their state, their nation, and around the world.

Today's economy has no geographic boundaries. It's an economy in which recruiting talent and resources is essential. Without them, cities fall behind. Montgomery has fallen behind.

It's time for us to look in the mirror. As we go forward, what must be done differently?

Throughout my adult life, I've tried to be part of changing Montgomery for the better. When I came home in 2004, I tried to build as many communities as I could. I believed that my future here was going to be in small business. I thought I would sit in the chamber of commerce as a business owner or as the owner of a franchise. I envisioned buying and selling franchises and growing those businesses and employing a lot of city residents.

And then something happened.

I'll use an analogy: I learned the hard way that, to get to the third base, you start by getting to first base.

With my first business, I had plans to get to third base and then home plate. We had plans for acquiring new franchises and scaling success across Montgomery and then the entire South.

But what we found is that we couldn't get to first and second base.

It didn't matter that we had a Columbia-educated engineer or an Auburn-educated architect or a Vanderbilt-educated MBA.

All of that went out the window when we couldn't raise capital or access technical assistance. It didn't matter how talented we were when the color of our skin implicitly held us back in the eyes of those who issue permits or make investment decisions.

Our success, or lack thereof, had ramifications for Montgomery's success. Montgomery isn't just competing against Birmingham, Huntsville, or Mobile; we're competing against Columbia, South Carolina; Richmond, Virginia; Chattanooga, Tennessee; and Louisville, Kentucky.

When you talk to political and business leaders in these cities, they'll tell you, "What we did fifteen years ago we aren't doing now. We are already thinking fifteen years down the line."

What are they doing? They're building a more inclusive economy, an opportunity economy that gives everyone the chance to achieve their level of success in every way possible. We need to recapture what we had on Monroe Street, here in Montgomery, prior to integration: a district with thriving minority and Black businesses and women-led organizations.

Many of the people with whom I've talked who are from Montgomery, don't see *that* Montgomery.

They don't see a Montgomery that's cohesive. They don't see a Montgomery that's collaborating, with government *and* business, Black *and* white residents, working together toward a set of shared goals.

Our success will instigate a reckoning for the state of Alabama, too. Looking ahead, 80 percent of America's jobs will be concentrated in our cities. In *The New Geography of Jobs*, Berkeley economist Enrico Moretti connects jobs and economic growth to the ability of a community to nurture and attract talent. Those that do so thrive. Those that do not attract new talent die on the vine. Cities are the front line of this revolution. Smaller towns and rural areas are getting smaller in population as young people migrate in greater numbers to our cities. Therefore, the question before us has to be: Who are we going to be as a city? Who are we going to be as a community? And what's going to be the narrative for Montgomery going forward?

The history and the headlines of our last mayoral election are fantastic. But it's here today, gone tomorrow. What people really want to see is change. They expect leadership throughout our entire community to do some things differently—not just politically but in the way we run our businesses, community associations, philanthropy, and nonprofits.

I believe that we can make that change happen together. I believe that because residents want their city to thrive.

To do so, we must start with the things that each of us can control. If we're willing to put aside our fears and have faith in one another, then we can begin to challenge the dogma of distrusting others merely because of the color of their skin that has held us back for years.

I'm under no illusion that the city would vote unanimously for this vision. I wouldn't win all the votes in my church or even in my own house.

But if Mayor James, who led a city of 163,000 people, had faith that we would reach 250,000 people by 1975, then there must have been optimism in our ability to come together across lines of difference. There must have been optimism in that City Hall. There must have been optimism in the city of Montgomery itself.

We must rediscover that optimism. We must work together in an unprecedented fashion to begin to move forward again as one city.

That will be hard. We must own our racial history. We must name and address the racial fault lines that have divided us and paralyzed us for decades.

We must understand the modern economy, work together, and be uncomfortable in our discussions and our actions. We owe our community discomfort. We owe it to those who shared Mayor James's vision fifty years ago. We owe it to those who will come after us to make the tough choices in the future. We must make sure we are not just celebrating our history—a bus boycott or, more recently, an election—but also have cause to celebrate our choices, the results, and the impacts they have on the lives of people who live in Montgomery and the surrounding river region.

✳ ✳ ✳

When I was in junior high school, I remember a guy who wanted to fight me because of something my dad did.

It was the early 1980s, and boom boxes were *in*. This was well before iPhones and AirPods. Sony Walkmans were only a few years on the market and far from widespread. Many of us were taking our cues from LL Cool J. (For the younger people reading this, go listen to Cool's *Radio* and check out the album's cover art.) Back then, people played their music loud for *everyone's* enjoyment—whether folks wanted it or not.

As a member of the city council, my dad was weighing a decision about whether to upgrade the noise ordinance as part of a crackdown on loud music, which was increasingly dominating the airwaves in neighborhoods and communities. Boom boxes weren't the only problem, of course: cars decked out with fancy booming stereo systems were all the rage, too. Up and down the streets of Montgomery, car stereos blared the latest hits. The proposal before the council would empower the police to ticket and heavily fine those blasting loud music.

The decision before the city council was a contentious one. And for middle school kids, the proposal was deeply unpopular. We loved boom boxes! We loved car stereos! We loved Cool J! We loved MJ! We loved Run-DMC! We were teenagers. The problem was I was being singled out for the council's expected decision to crack down on loud music. My dad was the council's most prominent leader, and everyone expected them to vote against fun. (At least, that's the way my classmates saw it.) In and out of class, my classmates gossiped that my dad was going to take away boom boxes and car stereos.

But here's the twist: my dad opted *not* to pass the ordinance. And that kid who wanted to fight? Well, he extended an olive branch after the decision. We actually became friends.

So, why do I share this? Well, because for all my work as mayor, I am, first and foremost, *a dad*. And it's never lost on me that my public life also affects the lives of my children. At their schools, they, too, must navigate and negotiate my decisions with their peers. I don't want to overstate it—this isn't a common occurrence; they're kids, after all, focused on the things all kids are consumed by—but I understand better than most how work in public life can impact a child whose father or mother is devoted to public service. It's inevitable and that's *real*. And while I share Mayor James's ambitions for Montgomery, there is no more important future that I personally cherish than that of my children.

Even in the most straightforward circumstances, being a dad isn't easy nor always simple. As a public servant, I've made the decision to devote myself to my family *and* my community. And every day I make choices between attending sports games for one of my boys or attending an important city council meeting. It's a constant push-pull. I carry that tension within me. It's a feeling to which a lot of dads can relate. And I don't always get it right. I know a lot of dads feel that way, too. But I try, every day, to be a good father to my college-age daughter and two young boys.

My daughter is thriving as a recent graduate of Howard. She was engaged in campus life, including and especially student politics. I am so proud of her. My boys need more of my time now as they approach middle and high school. And as with all things, I am better at some parts of the job of being a dad than at others. I obviously enjoy coaching my sons in sports and love supporting their aspirations in the arts. I have not enjoyed, however, middle school homework. And, like millions of other parents, I've discovered that I am not as smart as a fifth grader. There's a humility that parenthood introduces to your life. Some days I am reminded that I was never good at geometry. And while my boys think it's somewhat cool that I am mayor, it's far from a major fixation. They'd rather just have more time with their dad.

As two career-driven professionals, Tamika and I talk every day about my role in our boys' lives. Before I became mayor, our responsibilities as parents were more evenly shared. We would divide pickup and drop-off and take turns tackling homework and bedtime. Since I became mayor, Tamika has had to assume a lot more of the parenting in our house while balancing a career of her own. That is, of course, not uncommon. While our country has made strides toward gender equity, women continue to overwhelmingly pull more than their fair share in the running of our households. Women disproportionately shoulder the burdens of child-rearing and housework. I am profoundly grateful for Tamika's role in our lives as a mother to our children and I never take for granted all that she must sacrifice to do it. I bring that recognition to my job and believe our government must do more to support working families. We must push for a "care economy" that provides accessible childcare, universal pre-K, and paid family leave to help moms *and* dads step up in their households and in the lives of their children.

I've seen my sister confront similar gender dynamics: she is the oldest, with two younger brothers. A CPA by training, my sister is easily the smartest of the three of us. She was accepted to Princeton but chose HU. She's brilliant. She's a motivator, too. She's very encouraging of everyone in the family, always saying, "Hey, I knew you were going to be successful. I knew you would be successful."

There's a tinge of sadness in her words. My sister sacrificed a very successful corporate career to support my parents and tend to the family real estate business. Her work isn't glamorous. And she's not managing a real estate empire. She oversees a modest portfolio of rental properties that my parents started investing in decades ago. Taking that step to look after the family and support my parents in their later years could not have been easy, given my sister's talent and enormous accomplishment; she has sacrificed for the family unit. I admire that about her and recognize, daily, that she bears a cost, and tacitly her gender has played a role in that.

I name these things *because* they are uncomfortable and important. Our wives, mothers, sisters, and daughters deserve a society where they can pursue the full measure of their ambition without having to unfairly sacrifice. As a man, I wrestle with my own complicity in a system that must change. I am reminded that as far as we've come since the 1960s, we still have a long way to go until we realize a society that is truly equitable and fair.

As I try to fulfill my own parental responsibilities, I try to do my part, understanding that I am not carrying the same load as my sister or my wife. Nevertheless, I have a role to play. As a dad, I try to meet my children where they are. For my two young boys, a lot of times they just need a sounding board. Other times they need an instructor. As they come of age, they're figuring out their bodies, their friends, their interests—*who they are*. That requires me to engage them on their terms.

It's also important to me that they do not feel pressure to live up to their grandfather's name or their father's name. I know from my own upbringing how challenging that is. I had to leave Montgomery, travel the world, and try and fail and try again in business in order to forge an identity that was *mine*. My dad and his work loomed large in my life. As a parent, I try to protect space for my children to discover and forge their own identities, and I am careful when I pull them into my world. I try to teach them self-love, which begins with self-acceptance and the ability to set and enforce boundaries so that you have the space to grow into yourself. That can be hard for young Black boys who face a world that constantly sends messages about who they are while pulling them in too many directions—and not all of them good. For my part, as their father, I create space for them to focus on their outlets, the choices and activities that *they* want to make to advance their interests, their dreams, and their goals. I can relate to their desire to be independent and to exercise independence in ways that most resonate with them, and not necessarily with others. For me, my outlet was football. It was sports. On the field, I was my own man. You had to win or lose on your effort. It didn't matter who the other person was. You had to be able to do those things on your own. So I try to encourage my two boys to find their own ways to lead, to be themselves and excel.

Fatherhood is the most important leadership role I've ever had. It's an honor to raise young men who love and respect one another, their mother, and their grandparents and who aspire to contribute to the betterment of our community. And despite my own shortcomings, it energizes me to see them take a greater interest in the running of our household, their education, and their city. They're better than I was at that age—more engaged, and more aware—and as they embrace their leadership, they build on a legacy that has seen previous generations to brighter days.

Chapter 11

THE LESSONS

When I set out to write this book, my goal was to produce something more than a memoir. God willing, I have many more years left in my career and across my life. I hope and pray that my best days remain ahead of me. However, in this moment, it is important to chronicle the remarkable leadership and life lessons from our civil rights generation. Our country is fighting for its very soul, and it will take all of us to steer her to better days. To prepare for that fight, we must learn from the great leaders walking among us.

The civil rights generation isn't perfect. They are, however, a remarkable cohort of great Americans who have made an indelible impact on our city, state, and country. We should do everything we can to chronicle their stories and learn from their impact. I think about Montgomery legends Jo Ann Robinson, and Fred Gray, who was recently awarded the Presidential Medal of Freedom, for their extraordinary contribution to civil rights. I think about my mom and dad, who are still here and healthy. So many members of this generation have relevant wisdom to share with those leading and driving change today.

As I lead Montgomery through one of her hardest trials, I apply what I've learned from the civil rights generation every day. No doubt, the challenges confronting us are unique. But they are not altogether different from the massive problems my parents confronted in the 1950s and '60s: our democracy was buckling under the weight of segregation, and many of us, especially those of us advocating for Black equality, women's liberation, and LGBTQ rights, were fighting for very our lives. Stepping back, it's important to acknowledge that our struggle is an ancient one: we must marshal the good in all of us to fight against the forces of oppression. Nothing less than democracy and freedom are on the line.

As I reflect on my leadership journey and the work I do here in

Montgomery, here are a few of the leadership principles that I keep front and center.

LEADERSHIP ISN'T A POSITION; IT'S A CHOICE. AND LEADERS MAKE CHOICES EVERY DAY.

One of the biggest misconceptions about leadership is that it revolves, fundamentally, around someone's title or position. It doesn't. Leadership is about choices. I know a lot of people who sit in a big seat at a company or in a government office and they don't lead. And I know more people than I can count who hold no formal title or position and are wildly effective leaders.

I am often asked: What's it like to be the mayor? That question is quickly followed by another: What's it like to be a leader?

I reject the premise of the question. Every one of us confronts the decision to lead or not, every single day. The very best leaders view every choice through the prism of leadership, aware that their example reverberates to affect others. Gandhi never held a formal title or position, and throughout his public life he nevertheless transformed a nation and inspired civil rights movements worldwide, including in South Africa and the United States. Dr. King was similar. While he was president of the Southern Christian Leadership Conference, the organization he led was tiny compared to the gargantuan size of the movement he inspired.

For Gandhi and King, their commitment to *doing the right thing to achieve the right goal at the right time* no matter the personal cost is what inspired others to follow them to realize a bigger, bolder vision.

As mayor, I am committed to leading. I never take my community's support for granted. The fastest way to lose your followers? Believe your hype; take your public trust for granted. In the long run, great leaders are followed because of their choices. And good choices center community and the collective interest. I wake up every day committed to leading. And whether I am the mayor or not, that means making good leadership choices.

My dad's leadership commitment started at a young age. He made the choice to lead every time he saw others in need and made the decision to help. By always doing right by others, he led. That is the essence of leadership. No doubt, his upbringing in the Alabama Black Belt shaped him in powerful ways:

> *We grew up poor. I worked and the wages were low. Oftentimes, you worked and didn't get paid because somebody just asked you to come and "help me." You didn't ask what you were going to [be paid]. You just helped.*

In the Alabama Black Belt, Black communities, just decades out from the end of slavery, *had no choice but to pull together*. If they didn't share their resources in pursuit of their common goal, life was unlikely to improve. That culture shaped Black communities and that ethos showed up in the civil rights movement. The humblest of citizens—the domestic, the retail worker, the student, the retiree—all made leadership *choices* when they saw a need and decided to do something about it.

Rosa Parks kept her seat and in an instant contributed an act of leadership that changed the world.

Remember, any individual can lead because every individual confronts choices.

LEADERS EMBRACE DISCOMFORT.

Dr. King once said, "If you feel comfortable in your coalition, it's too small."

He was right. One of the hardest parts of leadership is the choice to work with others, even and especially when it's uncomfortable.

When I look across our social movements today, I worry that

we limit our progress *because we don't have a radical and expansive view of allyship*. When we fail to enlist the allies necessary to advance our cause—which means, in part, enduring discomfort by working with someone who doesn't see eye to eye with you on *everything*—we make a huge mistake, because we leave value on the table. Hanging together when there's shared interest to fight for a worthy cause is the *only* way *anything* has ever gotten done in this country.

Did the Founding Fathers agree with one another on everything? Nope. How about Abraham Lincoln and the Republican Party at the height of the Civil War? Of course not. Or Harriet Tubman and the women's suffrage movement, which had excluded if not altogether ignored Black women for much of the nineteenth century? No way.

But in all those examples, the leaders and their allies weathered discomfort, and often disagreement, to advance the greater good. The Founding Fathers agreed on the core tenets of the Revolution and created, very imperfectly, a nation dedicated to basic human rights. While he was alive, Abraham Lincoln was viewed as an insufferable moderate by his allies in the Republican Party. Yet they transformed a nation, abolishing slavery and embedding civil rights in the Constitution. And Harriet Tubman, through dogged determination, expanded the conversation in the women's suffrage movement to include Black women.

Closer to home, my dad modeled this principle throughout his entire career in education. As the most prominent Black leader in public education in Alabama, my dad made the controversial decision to merge his association with the white education association. Why? Because they were, unequivocally, stronger together. Naturally, many members of the two organizations didn't trust one another, and after the merger, Black and white membership plunged. Nevertheless, my dad and the leader of the white association, Paul

Hubbert, worked together without major incident for more than four decades. In the process, they rebuilt the membership and transformed working conditions for teachers and educators across the state. They also used education to galvanize progressives in conservative Alabama.

When asked about the merger, my dad shared what it meant to work through discomfort to serve the greater good:

We put together a coalition of Black and white teachers in the AEA. That was the organization's name, the Alabama Education Association. We put together a coalition. The executive secretary was white, a young fellow by the name of Paul R. Hubbert. Good fellow. He also believed that working folk had rights. He believed in it, and he called it a labor union. We combined the two into a strong political organization. I was not only the Executive Secretary at the teacher's organization, I was Chairman of the Alabama Democratic Conference.

I give Paul all the credit. He was a very good fella. I worked with him for 42 years . . . Paul was intelligent. Paul had read the scripture. I never saw Paul as a drumbeater for civil rights per se, but at no time, our whole career, the 42 years we were together, he ever tried to prevent me from defending the rights of our teachers, and our members. At no point.

"*I never saw Paul as a drumbeater for civil rights per se.*" What a statement. My dad is fanatical about civil rights, and yet he worked as closely as you can work with another human being although he did not share the same orientation.

That had to be uncomfortable.

And I know that my dad and Mr. Hubbert understood that they were indeed stronger together. They didn't necessarily share all the same priorities, but in the end *they shared the same interests*.

Knowing the difference between the two is key. As such, Paul stood with my dad when he advocated for civil rights in education. My dad stood with Paul to make sure the teaching profession and the interests of educators across the state, no matter their race, were protected.

Leadership isn't always comfortable. And the great leaders seek out discomfort by reaching their allies to grow their coalitions.

LEADERS REMAIN RIGHTEOUS.

If leadership is fundamentally about making the right choices, then sometimes the choice that leaders face is hard. Leaders face tremendous pressure to get it right as valid interests compete and often conflict. And frequently it's hard to know what right is. Usually, what's right is the decision that does the greatest good *over the long term*. Often a good long-term decision requires short-term sacrifice.

When COVID-19 swept across the state of Alabama, most of my coalition insisted that it was the wrong time to pursue a tax increase to invest in education:

"People are already sacrificing."

"Everyone is distracted by the public health crisis; you won't be able to break through the noise to make your case."

"You just got elected. Why not wait until later, when things are calmer and simpler?"

But as Dr. King said, "The time is always right to do the right thing." And as my father cautioned, "There's nothing politically right that's morally wrong," and those of us who are public stewards should "give our service but never our soul."

The education decision was a classic trade-off between the long and short term. By underinvesting in our children's future, we failed them for decades. And COVID-19 risked exacerbating the inequities that plagued too many of our communities. If we didn't act to invest in our children's education then, we risked losing them for all time. We would need to sacrifice in the short term for the long-term good.

COVID-19 plunged our country and communities into a moral crisis: What do we owe to one another when everyone's lives are threatened by an invisible foe? How do we consider investments in our future when the present is so fraught with danger?

Well, one of my dad's maxims is "The hottest place in hell is reserved for those who maintained their neutrality in a time of moral crisis." No doubt my dad's voice played in my head when we made the decision to do right by our children at the height of the pandemic. It was the righteous choice.

Expedient solutions are usually more popular because they almost always require less of us. But that doesn't make them right. And righteous decisions consider long-term costs and benefits.

The COVID-19 pandemic was full of dilemmas for those of us leading. And across the board, the expedient solution was to simply let everyone do what they wanted and to ask as little of the public as possible. But we've never endured through a crisis without pulling together, without shared sacrifice.

Effective leaders usually *know* the right thing to do. In public life, it's rare to encounter a genuine puzzle. Most of the time, the right answer is obvious; it's just hard. It's unpopular. The right choices demand shared sacrifice. But the right answer is usually clear.

When asked about what he learned from Dr. King, my dad shared the following:

> *What I learned from him was that this thing of nonviolence was very good, because he would speak about the fact that you couldn't fight back in your pursuit for fairness and justice, because the white folk had all the equipment for violence. They*

had the guns, they had the National Guard, they had every-
thing. And it happened this nonviolent movement, what we
had during the sit-ins, having this nonviolent movement was,
well, was very good in many ways. It saved a lot of lives. There's
number one. There were times when there were people, I'm cer-
tain who would fight back. But it saved a lot of lives, and it also
"handcuffed" those who would perpetuate violence. That they
didn't have an excuse to shoot you.

I love this insight because *nonviolence was hard.* And Dr. King
was under enormous pressure throughout his life to condone and
allow violence. That would have been expedient. But it wouldn't
have been right.

Leaders remain righteous.

LEADERS LEVERAGE MOMENTUM.

Making the righteous choice does not mean forging ahead blindly
or without respect to political costs. Effective leaders often work
incrementally so that they don't lose their followers. You can lead
only if others follow. Striking the right balance between the short
and long term speaks to the art of leadership.

In navigating that art, the greatest leaders—Dr. King, Cesar
Chavez—understood that momentum is *everything.* The civil rights
movement was, for example, a series of incremental steps—"direct
actions," like the sit-ins, protests, and marches, and "campaigns"
like the Montgomery bus boycott—that were oriented toward building and leveraging momentum.

Momentum was key because the civil rights movement, like
all social movements, started small. If Dr. King had tried to get
landmark legislation passed from the outset, he would have failed.
Instead, he nurtured a vision that grew from a few followers into a
mass movement. Along the way, he grew his coalition through a

series of what famed organizer Marshall Ganz calls "little wins." In *Why David Sometimes Wins*, Ganz chronicles all the ways King, Chavez, and, later, Obama organized a series of little wins that built momentum for their movement.

Often, when we look back on the March on Washington and the landmark civil rights legislation that passed in 1964 and 1965, it's easy to view those "big wins" as inevitable. History always looks inevitable in retrospect. But the truth is any big win was the result of direct actions that were often small and involved a relatively small group of people. Those actions built on one another until the movement reached a tipping point when the big wins came within reach.

I often counsel young people who want to change the world to *just start*. Start somewhere. Find a few friends—and a few allies—and achieve a little win. Celebrate that victory and get others to pay attention to it. Enlist more friends and allies. Achieve another victory. And so on.

Dramatic change rarely happens overnight.

It's often the result of painstaking, calculated effort. Those incremental steps ultimately add up to create the window for big change.

As my dad says, "Remember, what goes around comes around. No army is stronger than an idea whose time has come. It is better to make change afraid than to be afraid of change."

LEADERSHIP > EFFECTIVENESS.

One of the underappreciated aspects of the civil rights movement was that the organizations that represented the backbone of the movement—like the Southern Christian Leadership Conference (Dr. King's organization) and the Student Nonviolent Coordinating Committee (the student organization that first involved my father and mother in the movement)—were *small*, with revenues of less than $200,000 at their peaks. In 1966, the SCLC had revenues of a little less than $170,000; it had expenses of roughly $215,000.[1]

You read that right. The SCLC operated at a loss. *And it wasn't that much money.*

In 2022 dollars, accounting for inflation, $215,000 is just less than $2 million.

SNCC was even smaller. Both organizations were scrappy and thinly staffed. Stretched beyond its means, SNCC wasn't always effective or particularly organized.

Yet these organizations and the movement of volunteers they inspired changed the country.

Why?

Because *leadership is greater than effectiveness.* Effectiveness matters, but leadership matters much more. The civil rights movement was resource-poor but leadership-rich. *That* was the difference maker.

Now, to be clear, I am not advocating for bad management or encouraging you to neglect good operations. As a leader, if I am known for *anything*, it's a commitment to results, good management, and a fidelity to data-driven decision-making. That is all hugely important. But it's more important to remember that there's no substitute for great leadership, and generally that's all that effective social movements have to work with.

When my dad started in the civil rights movement, he started as a student at ASU. Here's what he said when asked about it:

I was involved in the sit-in movement in 1960. I was put on probation by the government, by the State Board of Education of Alabama, and that's the probation for attempting to desegregate the Montgomery County Courthouse. That time, Alabama State was under the State Board of Education, and the Gover-

nor demanded that we be disciplined. Those of us who had Alabama addresses were put on probation, those who had out-of-state addresses were expelled.

The case went to federal court in Montgomery. The District Court ruled in favor of the state, that the state had the power to do what it did, to expel and put us on probation. The case was appealed to the Fifth Circuit Court of Appeals. At that time, Alabama was in the fifth circuit; it's in the 11th circuit now. The Fifth Circuit overruled the District Court, sent the case back.

And so, the students who were expelled were eventually eligible for readmittance. Those of us who were on probation . . . the case had been reversed. That was 1960. I was an organizer of the SNCC, Student Nonviolent Coordinating Committee. We organized that group on Easter weekend, 1960 in Raleigh, North Carolina, at Shaw University. That's where SNCC was born.

When my dad started organizing, there was no student government or any student group whose purpose was to fight for civil rights. They were just a group of young people trying to make a difference. And even after the state of Alabama threw the book at them—expelled them, put them on probation for trying to desegregate the courthouse—they found other friends and allies and kept at it. Their search for other friends and allies brought them to North Carolina, where they, along with 126 other students, gave life to a new organization, SNCC.

SNCC was a breakthrough for the civil rights movement, and the involvement of young people was a change from previous iterations of the movement. Dr. King traveled to North Carolina and spoke there as SNCC was getting off the ground. He said to the students, "What is new in your fight is the fact that it was initiated, fed, and sustained by students."

SNCC was conceived and founded by the great Ella Baker. And when you account for who participated in that initial organizing effort in North Carolina, the roster is astonishing: Diane Nash, John Lewis, Marion Barry, Stokely Carmichael, Julian Bond, my dad. SNCC fueled so much of the movement because it mobilized the people. It also seeded the movement's leadership. Those students would all grow up to be leaders of the first order.

All of it started humbly, with little structure and virtually no resources. And yet it grew into a powerhouse.

All of it is a testament to leadership.

LEADERS SACRIFICE.

As my dad always said, there are too many people who want to wear the crown but aren't willing to bear the cross.

A hallmark of leadership is sacrifice. Invariably, sacrifice is needed to achieve the larger objective. You may well find that achieving something significant is at odds with your own personal aims, objectives, and interests. You don't have to look far across the civil rights movement to observe sacrifice.

When I was a child, there were many nights when my dad was on the road for his job. Sometimes he took us with him, but usually he went alone, leaving my mother to hold it all together. It was a lot for her. And for him. For both, it was a sacrifice.

Some leaders, like Dr. King, paid the ultimate price. Others incurred a less obvious cost. I think about Hank Aaron, one of my heroes. Hank grew up in Mobile, Alabama, where he, along with seven siblings, used to hide under the bed when the KKK marched down the street in front of his home and burned crosses in his neighborhood. At the young age of thirteen, Hank heard Jackie Robinson speak. Jackie broke baseball's color barrier in 1947 and went out of his way to inspire young Black ballplayers. Thanks to Jackie, Hank was determined to play Major League ball. For five years he played in the Negro leagues before he was acquired by the Braves organization, where he broke the color barrier in Georgia's minor league system.

Just like Jackie, he was the first.

And just like Jackie, he endured death threats and hate mail throughout his career. Racist sneers and taunts followed wherever he played. The necessary precautions were suffocating. Hank would exit the stadium through the back doors to avoid the menacing crowds. And he always required a police escort. One year, the U.S. Postal Service awarded him a plaque as the recipient of the most mail in the country. He got so much mail that the Braves hired a full-time employee just to comb through the nearly 1 million pieces that arrived that year—a lot of it, but not all of it, was hate mail.

Hank endured all that to *play baseball*. But it wasn't just about baseball. He endured all that to play baseball as a path-breaking Black man. To set an example just like his hero, Jackie Robinson.

Hank's treatment in the league reached a fevered pitch in 1974 when he broke Babe Ruth's home run record. Hank often remarked that the incessant threats to his life, the jeering, and the psychic weight of constantly staying vigilant robbed the joy of baseball from him. When he ended the season in 1973, just short of the home run record, he said his biggest fear was not being able to live to see the next season.

Hank played deep into his career because he knew what it meant to achieve the sport's ultimate accomplishment as a Black man. He knew that his success would help silence the racist arguments about Black inferiority that still swirled in the popular culture, even in the 1970s. Hank sacrificed for the movement. His leadership role, much like Jackie Robinson's, was to endure and prove Black excellence for the world to witness day in and day out.

Leadership is dangerous. Anytime you're trying to change things, you put yourself at risk. The bigger the change, the bigger the risk. Leaders do it anyway. They sacrifice.

TRUST IS EVERYTHING, AND REMEMBER: EVERYTHING IS PERSONAL.

For my parents, trust is everything.

My dad was always emphatic: "Let your handshake be your contract and your word your bond." In his work, he also rejected the notion that politics was inherently deceitful or somehow dishonest. He was clear that "some folks say politics is dirty. Politics is a noble profession. It's 'politricks' that's dirty."

I learned early on from my parents that telling the truth and living honestly was *the* most important thing. More important than sports. Even more important than grades. Character matters. And the only way to really discern character is to pay attention to what people *do* over long stretches of time. As we got older and made new friends, my dad would always caution, "Watch what people do rather than listen to what they say." When I started out in politics, he took it a step further. He stressed the importance of paying attention to incentives—the forces that work on people and raise the risk of distorting their behavior and challenging their character.

One of my favorite sayings of his took me years to truly understand: "Keep in mind that you can't send for your lunch by way of a hungry boy. He'll eat it! Leaders who are hungry are greedy. They'll let their stomachs prevail over their principles." In politics, elected officials who are struggling to hold on to their seat or raise money for their next campaign are vulnerable. In my coalition, I try to support my peers in the fight. I don't take their support for granted and I appreciate that it's easier to hang together when everyone is fortified in their interests. That may not feel good, but it's a reality. And an important one.

My dad's attitude toward trust carried over to his relationships. My father is nothing if not loyal. He would always say, "Make new friends but never leave an old friend in order to make a new one. Nothing is more painful than betrayal by a person who you believed was once your friend."

Finally, part of loyalty is gratitude and appreciation. It is important to remember who had your back and who showed up when it mattered most. "Of all crimes, the worst crime is ingratitude."

LEADERS CREATE LEADERS.

One of the enduring hallmarks of leadership is the creation of other leaders.

The ultimate responsibility of leaders is to inspire leadership in others. That's how we scale our efforts to change the world. There is no other way. None of us can change the world alone.

Dr. King modeled this principle. After he was tragically struck down, his legacy, the movement, continued. When my dad was asked about the assassination of Dr. King, here's what he shared:

We were all devastated when we lost Dr. King. We were devastated. We were all hurt. But then, we had said all the time long before that, really, if you jail the son's father, the son is going to come along. If you jail Martin Luther King, you'll have a John Lewis.

When Dr. King died, while he was serving in the midst of his Poor People's Campaign, he was focused on advancing the economic agenda, but he had not abandoned the cause of civil rights. He started encouraging folks to run for office. And so, we were beginning to take advantage of the 1965 Voting Rights Act. We were beginning to run candidates that Martin King called "whites of goodwill" to put in office. We were ... even getting a different kind of Black [leader] to run for office. When Dr. King died, back in 1968, that was the first year that I became a delegate to the Democratic Convention.

We doubled down. Of course, Ralph Abernathy took Martin's place, and Ralph was a very courageous and good man. But the movement was taking shape. The benefits of the Selma to Montgomery March were paying off. How was it paying off? We had a 1965 Voting Rights Act. We had delegates in the Democratic Convention. But it was the beginning of the political drive as well. You see, because our fight has been in several places: education, economic, and political.

And so, in 1968, we had the big fight in Chicago, where we were very much involved in the thrust to enjoy the benefits of the Voting Rights Act. It had not expanded like it is now. Of course, when Dr. King died, we didn't give up.

"*When Dr. King died, we didn't give up.*" The leaders around Dr. King continued to push. They pushed the civil rights movement into new, vital areas of progress: the fight for elected political representation, economic justice, equal education.

While they fought, my dad's generation also instilled in my generation a value system to guide our choices and decisions. It's the same value system that I am passing down to my children's generation. It's not important that every generation makes *exactly the same* decisions as their ancestors would standing in their shoes. After all, a new generation brings a fresh perspective and, usually, a better way of doing things. But grounding the next generation in enduring truths is the only way to ensure that the hard-earned wisdom of freedom fighters past guides those of us in the fight today.

When asked about the most pressing issues facing my generation, my dad emphasized the importance of that value system:

What are the issues for Steven's generation? First of all, keep our value system. Keep the value you learned with. Right. Keep that going.

I try to do for the children, and I think it's very crucial to every parent . . . I try to live by example, to teach them, and show them. I try to live by example, that's point one. But I've always believed that we've got to live by example. I don't think anybody has more influence on children than their parents.

They may do something different.

You can't sit there and say, "Look, I want my son to be a bishop." And he doesn't want to do that. You just have to accept what he wants to be. But you have to set the example. So we set the example.

That's the key.

And teach them honor.

And integrity.

That is so important. If you can teach your child your value system.

They might not do everything you want them to do, like you would do it. And they shouldn't. But we've taught them a value system.

And take trips; we'd take them with us, sometimes. Or most of the time, really, particularly during the summers.

I drove Steven all around this state. That's exactly right. And it helped him. And I told him when he was little, "You might not understand now, but one day, you will see it."

I think that our children got to still be impressed upon our values. They've got to understand that they are still Black. And they've got to understand that while we have made a lot of progress—and put me on the side of those who think we've made a lot of progress—we still have a lot left to do.

I think we'll continue to make progress.

My hope is built on the young white children. Those young-sters, they are more prone to be objective. And they balance things out. Our hope got to be built on the young whites, and the young Blacks, who go to school together, who wind up pray-ing together, playing together. That's where it will come. And that's when we'll be able to "cross the river of Jordan together."

ACKNOWLEDGMENTS

First, Best is only possible because of the sacrifice and strength of so many people who have lifted me throughout my life. There are countless people who have helped shape me along the way. To all who have played some part in who I am today and what may lie ahead, I say, thank you.

To my parents, Joe and Mollie, who instilled so much in me and continue to inspire me to this very day. Their faith in God; each other; and Irva, Joe, and me has been a source of strength that has sustained and shaped me into the man that I am as well as the man I still aspire to be. I cannot overstate the power of their example in my life. I am grateful to God above that I am their son.

My wife and children have had to sacrifice so many things so that we can serve our community. The magnitude of their sacrifice is not lost on me. The time that you never get back. In addition to my responsibilities as mayor, I added writing a book. It's hard enough sharing time and space of your husband with the public, but it's even more daunting when the remaining time must be shared with a project as time-consuming as writing a book. Through it all, Tamika has exhibited extraordinary support. Tamika, I am so thankful for your strength and our partnership.

For those who served as examples of "First, Bests" during my journey, I am eternally grateful. Those whose courage led them to stand in the breach at a much more tumultuous time so that I could serve today is a tribute to their work and legacy. To the men and women who have gone on to glory but who were there to share a pearl of wisdom at a church, tell a story at a political gathering, or stand silently in support for a cause—I lead and serve in your honor.

To my aunts and uncles, friends, cousins, classmates, fraternity brothers, mentors, and chat group posse, your encouragement cannot be understated. I hope this book serves as a barometer of our hopes, dreams, and lessons learned that we may pass on to future generations.

My heartfelt thanks go out to my campaign and mayor's staff who supported me in this journey: Chip Hill, Jamyla Philyaw, Tracie Davis, Denetra Shannon, Dina Campbell, Tania Johns, Phillip Ensler, Sheretha Gordon, Christian Crawford, Eddie Compton, and Meredith Lilly.

To Fagan Harris, I say thank you for helping me put my thoughts and experiences onto paper. I appreciate the spirit in which you approached this work from the very beginning. Your intellect and interest have brought about a compilation of lessons that I have only recently started to appreciate. I truly have reflected on the questions, statements, and imagery that you have made vivid in this book. It has truly been a joy to work with you, and I know greater work lies ahead.

All of this would have been for naught but for Penguin Random House and my editor, Joanna Ng. Her commitment to this project has been a staple of our success. No detail is too small, and her optimism about what we were putting together provided me with even more encouragement. Her patience with my schedule and responsibilities as mayor has been a relief because of the pressure it removed from the work.

I cannot speak enough about everyone on the Penguin Random House team. You have truly given me the juice that was needed to put everything into this project. Your excitement elicited more confidence as we went along in the various stages of writing this book.

I cannot say this with enough emphasis, but I want to thank my agent, Traci Smith, for her vision for what she saw in my story and election. Her insight to believe someone would want to read about my journey led to her reaching out to a colleague at CSE and friend and former college teammate of mine, Bobby Height. Their advice in taking this from idea to implementation has been a lesson in patience and professionalism. They connected me with Peter McGuigan, who was a great champion for this book as well. I cannot thank them enough.

A number of my great friends, including Charles L. Fischer III, Terrence Chavis, Aisha Francis-Samuels, and Ravi Howard, took the time to read the manuscript and offer suggestions, comments, and additional perspective. Their assistance in what to look for in a coauthor was invaluable, as was their confidence in the sharing of the narrative.

This book was an unseen blessing born out of my life experiences and historic electoral victory to lead my hometown of Montgomery, Alabama. I will always be thankful for those who believed in me from the very beginning and have shown such encouragement to get me to this point. It is an honor to represent you.

To my daughter and sons, I am filled with gratitude to have been blessed with you as my children, and I will forever pray that I will be to you what my mother and father have been to me.

Finally, I want to acknowledge and lift up every young person striving to make the most of their lives and to make a difference in their community. This book is for you, the next generation. Thank you for the inspiration to serve and sacrifice as we build and pass on a legacy that is committed to making America all that she can be. Together, let us continue in the work as, together, we forge a more perfect union.

NOTES

Chapter 1: Origins

1.   Martin Luther King, Jr., *I've Been to the Mountaintop* (San Francisco: HarperSanFrancisco, 1994).

2.   President Obama's commencement address at Rutgers University on May 15, 2016.

3.   Eric Foner, *Freedom's Lawmakers: A Directory of Black Officeholders during Reconstruction*, revised ed. (Baton Rouge: Louisiana State University Press, 1996), xi–xxxii.

4.   Vanessa Siddle Walker, *The Lost Education of Horace Tate: Uncovering the Hidden Heroes Who Fought for Justice in Schools* (New York: New Press, 2018).

5.   Tavis Smiley, "The One Single Thing Donald Trump and Martin Luther King, Jr. Have in Common," *Time*, December 1, 2017, https:// time.com/5042070/donald-trump-martin-luther-king-mlk/.

Chapter 2: The Mothers of the Movement

1.   Juanita J. Chinn, Iman K. Martin, and Nicole Redmond, "Health Equity among Black Women in the United States," *Journal of Women's Health* 30, no. 2 (February 2021): 212–19, https://www.ncbi .nlm.nih.gov/pmc/articles/PMC8020496/.

Chapter 4: More Than Race

1.   Ana Hernández Kent and Lowell R. Ricketts, "Has Wealth Inequality in America Changed over Time? Here Are Key Statistics," Federal Reserve Bank of St. Louis, December 2, 2020, https://www.stlouisfed

.org/open-vault/2020/december/has-wealth-inequality-changed-over
-time-key-statistics.

2. https://www.americanrhetoric.com/speeches/rfkcapetown.htm

3. https://www.americanrhetoric.com/speeches/rfkcapetown.htm

Chapter 7: Epiphany

1. John Lewis with Brenda Jones, *Across That Bridge: A Vision for Change and the Future of America* (New York: Hachette, 2012).

Chapter 11: The Lessons

1. Jesse B. Blayton, Letter to Dr. Martin L. King, Jr., June 30, 1966, crmvet.org/docs/660630_sclc_scope-fin.pdf.

ABOUT THE AUTHOR

STEVEN L. REED is the first Black mayor of Montgomery, Alabama, the birthplace of the modern civil rights movement, where he was born and raised. He has also served as the youngest and first Black person elected probate judge, Montgomery County's highest administrative position. Reed earned a bachelor of arts degree cum laude from Morehouse College and a master of business administration from Vanderbilt University's Owen Graduate School of Management. He and his wife, Tamika, are the proud parents of three children.